Edith Stein:
St. Teresa Benedicta of the Cross

María Ruiz Scaperlanda

Edith Stein

The Life and Legacy of St. Teresa Benedicta of the Cross

SOPHIA INSTITUTE PRESS
Manchester, New Hampshire

This book was originally published in 2001 by Our Sunday Visitor, Huntington, Indiana. This 2017 edition by Sophia Institute Press includes minor revisions. Permission to use material from other books was given for the original edition; see the special acknowledgments for details.

Printed in the United States of America. All rights reserved.

Cover design by Coronation Media.

On the cover: Barbed wire fence and wall (11920666) © Paul Prescott / shutterstock.com. Photo of Edith Stein taken from *Edith Stein: Her Life in Photos and Documents* (ICS Publications, Washington, DC).

Sophia Institute Press
Box 5284, Manchester, NH 03108
1-800-888-9344

www.SophiaInstitute.com

Sophia Institute Press® is a registered trademark of Sophia Institute.

Library of Congress Cataloging-in-Publication Data

Names: Scaperlanda, María Ruiz, 1960- author.
Title: Edith Stein : the life and legacy of St. Teresa Benedicta of the Cross / María Ruiz Scaperlanda.
Description: Manchester, New Hampshire : Sophia Institute Press, 2017. | Includes index.
Identifiers: LCCN 2017023090 | ISBN 9781622824649 (pbk. : alk. paper)
Subjects: LCSH: Stein, Edith, Saint, 1891-1942. | Carmelite Nuns—Germany—Biography. | Catholic converts—Germany—Biography. | Women philosophers—Germany—Biography. | Jews—Germany—Biography.
Classification: LCC BX4705.S814 S33 2017 | DDC 282.092 [B]—dc23 LC record available at https://lccn.loc.gov/2017023090

First printing

For Michael, my best friend, with all my love

Contents

Acknowledgments

A book like this one would not be possible without the help of many people along the way.

I owe much gratitude to the editors and translators of Edith Stein's works, who have made her work accessible to us: Mary Catherine Baseheart, L. Gelber, Josephine Koeppel, O.C.D., Romaeus Leuven, O.C.D., Michael Linssen, O.C.D., Maria Amata Neyer, O.C.D., Freda M. Oben, Walter Redmond, Marianne Sawicki, Waltraut Stein, and John Sullivan, O.C.D. Many thanks to Wally Redmond, who took the time to answer my questions, and special thanks to Sister Josephine Koeppel, O.C.D., of the Elysburg, Pennsylvania, Carmel, for her time, consultation, and expert advice. Thank you to the Discalced Carmelite community worldwide, who have preserved the writings, the faith, and the charism of Sister Teresa Benedicta of the Cross. Your work is a blessing to the Catholic community at large.

I am especially grateful to my own local Carmel, the Discalced Carmelite nuns in Piedmont, Oklahoma, who have supported this project by their faithful prayers. A special thanks to Sister Jeanne Marie Futrell for her copyediting and to Sister Ruth Miriam Irey, whose expertise in Jewish studies and on

Edith Stein: St. Teresa Benedicta of the Cross

Edith Stein was an invaluable aid to the development of this project.

Words of thanks are insufficient to express how grateful I am to Susanne Batzdorff, Edith Stein's niece, for her help and assistance in taking the time to read and comment on my work in progress. Your perspective and vision are unparalleled.

Profound thanks to Dr. Ilse Kerremans, who not only shared with me her personal devotion to Edith, but also welcomed me to Ghent, Belgium, to participate and learn from the 1998 Edith Stein Exhibit. Thank you, Ilse, for your help and support for the last two years, and for even becoming a translator for this project! A grateful tribute to Father Frans Hoornaert, O.C.D., the curator of the Ghent exhibit, and to Prior Piet Hoornaert, O.C.D., and the Carmelite friars in Ghent. Thank you for your warm hospitality and friendship.

Through Dr. Kerremans (and with the assistance of cyber-space!), I have come to "know" Father Michael Linssen, O.C.D., Director of the International Edith Stein Institute in Würzburg, Germany. Thank you, Father Michael, for being one of the work-in-progress readers and for agreeing to write a preface to the biography.

My family thanks the community of Carmel Maria vom Frieden in Köln for their generous hospitality during our Jubilee Year visit. Sister Carla Jungels and the rest of the community received our brood of six with open arms and loving hearts. And my interview with Sister Maria Amata Neyer added new insight to my understanding of their fellow Carmelite Edith Stein.

I must also thank my friend, fellow writer, and cyber-office mate, Colleen Smith, who strongly suggested that I pursue this project, as well as the editorial committee of Our Sunday Visitor, particularly Jacquelyn Lindsey, Editorial Development Manager,

Acknowledgments

for their vision in presenting an up-to-date biography of this great saint.

And finally, above all, this project would not have been possible without the love, patience, and encouragement of my children—Christopher, Anamaria, Rebekah, Michelle—and my home editor and husband, Michael. You all are awesome, and I love you.

Foreword

Edith Stein, Jewish by origin, lived her life for the greater part in the first half of the twentieth century. She graduated summa cum laude in 1916 with a doctorate in philosophy but was increasingly impeded in the practice of science due to the fact that she was a woman and a Jewess. Yet, by her publications and lectures, she became a famous personality in and outside Germany. Finally, however, together with countless others she was coerced by the Nazis to abandon her work in public.

Under circumstantial compulsion, she could freely fulfill a longtime cherished desire: she became a nun in the Carmel convent in Cologne, taking the name Sister Teresa Benedicta of the Cross. The "open" world became for her a closed world, a world that locked her out. She opened for herself a future in the hidden privacy of a convent. What in the opinion of many is to be buried alive was, for her, a new beginning of an authentic life toward eternal Being and eternal Truth. To the outside world she would have remained hidden in her freely chosen concealment if she hadn't become, as did millions of others, a sacrifice in the horrible center of the history of mankind, the *Shoah*. Her body was merged with the anonymity of the massacre. But her spirit lived on through the people who got acquainted with her and who learned to appreciate her through her many writings, which have been preserved.

Edith Stein was beatified in 1987. In 1998, she was canonized. A large number of her writings are published and have been translated into many languages. A critical edition of her complete works (at this writing) has been started. Her name and her teachings, her person and her vision, have become well known to many people. She is respected and esteemed. For many of us she is a safe guide in an unsafe world.

In this situation, I welcome the publication of this Edith Stein biography, written by María Ruiz Scaperlanda. In this biography, the life of Edith Stein is opened for the contemporary reader with great empathy in her fundamental genuine honesty, a rich life despite precarious circumstances due to time and cultural circumstances. Along with these subjects, the biography explores Edith's search for her own identity along with the relationship between Judaism and Christianity.

María Ruiz Scaperlanda opens for us in her book a human life in essence supported and guided by God, the hidden and increasingly revealing, rich, and enriching life of St. Edith Stein.

—Michael Linssen, O.C.D.
Director of the International Edith Stein Institute
Würzburg, Germany
(Translated by Dr. Ilse Kerremans)

Introduction

This concise biographical account of Edith Stein is based on the writings by and about her in English, notably her autobiographical memoir, *Life in a Jewish Family*, and *Self-Portrait in Letters*, both published by ICS, and *Edith Stein: Selected Writings* as well as my book *Aunt Edith: The Jewish Heritage of a Catholic Saint*, published by Templegate. Throughout this book, Ms. Scaperlanda makes a conscientious effort to present different points of view side by side, thus giving a multifaceted portrait of Edith Stein as seen by scholars, friends, and relatives, by Catholics and Jews alike. This affords the readers an insight into the complex aspects of her life and death, as well as the impact of her character and personality on those who knew her. It may motivate them to delve deeper into the abundant literature, some of which has been liberally quoted in this work.

My own relationship to Edith derives from the fact that she was my aunt, the sister of my mother, Erna Biberstein, née Stein. Of the seven brothers and sisters in the Stein family, my mother outlived all the others, and, in the end, it was she who became the link not only to Edith Stein's other family, her Carmelite Sisters, but also to those who admired her, studied her writings, and finally those who worked on the long process for her can-onization. When my mother died in 1978, at the age of almost eighty-eight, the large collection of books and documents and the task of corresponding with the ever-increasing number of Edith's admirers and scholars devolved upon me and has been an ongoing task and challenge ever since.

I have seen it as my duty to follow in my mother's footsteps in seeking to preserve honesty and integrity in the manner in which my aunt's life and character are portrayed in the media. Fre-quently, I consider it my duty to contact authors for the purpose of calling attention to errors and outright misrepresentations. I have come in contact with a large circle of people in many parts of the world, with whom I maintain an ongoing correspondence, in some cases, a lively exchange of ideas and information, and in a few, even friendship.

Most important, these activities have led to what I consider the most significant aspect of my involvement: they have helped to build bridges of understanding and friendship among people of different faiths and nationalities, to encourage a greater openness to learning about one another, and, through getting to know each other, to create respect and a willingness to draw closer for the important task of *tikkun olam*, "creating a better world."

We may debate whether Edith Stein was murdered in the *Shoah* because of her Jewish origins or gave her life as a martyr for the Faith she had embraced in midlife; but ultimately we can find, in remembering her, our common humanity and the resolve to make sure that the atrocities that cost her her life must never again be allowed to happen upon this earth. Then we will not only honor the memory of Edith Stein but also take an important step for-ward for the benefit of humankind. I have found that this message resonates with the various Edith Stein societies that I have visited or corresponded with: in Wroclaw, the former Breslau, birthplace of Aunt Edith and also of myself; Lubliniec, birthplace of my mother and my grandmother; the Edith Stein Guild of America, based in New York; and the Edith Stein Society of Germany. This message also resonates with the Carmelite Sisters in Cologne who preserve her archives and her memory; the Edith Stein Carmel in Tübingen, which took its name from her and feels therefore that it has a special bond to her; and the Carmelite communities in various places that it has been my privilege to visit and get acquainted with.

Twice in recent years we visited the city of Wroclaw, Poland, formerly Breslau, Germany, where, after the fall of the Iron Curtain, an Edith Stein Society was founded. It set itself the goal of creating better relations between Catholics and Jews and between Poles and Germans. We had many conversations with these very sincere people. Having seen the consequences of confrontation and hate, they want to pursue peace and understanding. Their problem is that the Jews of Wroclaw are suspicious of them and distrust them when they are approached under the banner of Edith Stein.

"How can we gain their trust?" the members of the Society asked us. "Why is it so hard to get closer to them?"

To us Jews it is obvious that for Jews, Edith Stein cannot be a bridge and can thus not be viewed as a role model. Jews see her as someone who left Judaism and joined a different faith community. Catholics, however, see her in a different light. She is, to them, a bridge to Judaism, because she is a "daughter of Israel," descended from a Jewish family. She also personifies, for Christians, the millions of victims of the Holocaust. To Jews, the Holocaust assumes shape and individuality because almost every Jewish family has relatives who perished in the Holocaust.

Edith Stein: St. Teresa Benedicta of the Cross

Our advice to the Edith Stein Society of Wroclaw was to approach the Jewish community, not in the name of their patron saint, but simply in order to gain their cooperation for some common projects that they can accomplish together. By collaborating on worthy causes they can get to know one another better and establish friendships that may open doors to further dialogue.

In October 2000, I was invited to participate in a program at the Vatican pavilion at the World Expo 2000 in Hannover. October 3, which is observed in Germany as the Day of German Unity, has also, somewhat significantly, been dedicated to the theme of Judaism and Christianity by the apostolic nuncio. Edith Stein is once again seen as a bridge to facilitate dialogue between Christians and Jews, and I was able to play a part in this meaningful event.

It certainly shows that we have made progress in our rapprochement.

The honors bestowed on Edith Stein have also strengthened our family bonds, for the canonization ceremony on October 11, 1998, brought together approximately one hundred members of our family from the four corners of the earth, a remarkable experience and the beginning of many new connections and friendships.

If Edith Stein has been the catalyst for all this, it is clear that she still exerts a strong influence on the generations of her family, most of whom never knew her.

It is a privilege for me, as one of the few surviving individuals who knew my beloved aunt and remember her, to extend my good wishes to the writer of this book, who has immersed herself in the study of Edith Stein and is here sharing her insights with her readership.

—Susanne M. Batzdorff

Part 1

Edith Stein's Sainthood

Chapter 1

⌒

Edith Stein's Journey to Sainthood

At the end of her life, Edith Stein considered herself one of the countless "hidden souls" who are part of the invisible Church and who regularly remain hidden from the whole world. She was a contemplative nun, a member of the Discalced Carmelite Order.

Yet, as Edith herself pointed out, throughout the history of humankind the visible Church has grown out of this invisible one. In the Old Testament, as the patriarchs allowed themselves to be used as God's pliant instruments, "[God] established them in an external visible efficacy as bearers of historical development." And every one of the events and persons who intertwined in the mystery of the Incarnation—Mary, Joseph, Zechariah, Elizabeth, the shepherds, the kings, Simeon, and Anna—had behind them "a solitary life with God and were prepared for their special tasks before they found themselves together in those awesome encounters and events." To most hidden souls, their impact and affinity can remain hidden even from themselves and others for their entire lives, Edith wrote the year before her death.

> But it is also possible for some of this to become visible in the external world. . . . The deeper a soul is bound

to God, the more completely surrendered to grace, the stronger will be its influence on the form of the church. Conversely, the more an era is engulfed in the night of sin and estrangement from God, the more it needs souls united to God. And God does not permit a deficiency. The greatest figures of prophecy and sanctity step forth out of the darkest night.... Certainly the decisive turning points in world history are substantially co-determined by souls whom no history book ever mentions. And we will only find out about those souls to whom we owe the decisive turning points in our personal lives on the day when all that is hidden is revealed.[1]

During one of the darkest periods of our human history, deeply rooted in this "estrangement from God" and "the night of sin" and death that she describes, Edith Stein chose to take on the name of Sister Teresa Benedicta of the Cross and to unite her soul to God fully and completely as a contemplative nun. Surely, this is no coincidence.

This is Edith Stein's legacy.

Long before Pope John Paul II proclaimed Sister Teresa Benedicta of the Cross a saint in the Catholic Church in 1998, the "hidden life" of Edith Stein had become known and remembered in faith communities, mostly throughout Europe. This hidden soul and her complete trust in divine grace became slowly visible to the external world, as Catholics throughout that continent recognized the unparalleled, deliberate, and brilliant legacy left behind by the interior life of this woman of Jewish descent who

---

[1] Edith Stein, *The Hidden Life: Hagiographic Essays, Meditations, Spiritual Texts*, ed. L. Gelber and Michael Linssen, O.C.D., trans. Waltraut Stein (Washington, DC: ICS Publications, 1992), 109–110.

fell in love with Truth and transformed her entire life because of that encounter with Jesus Christ. Her surrender to grace is all the more visible because of the dark night that enveloped the period of history in which she lived—and died—years when millions of men and women were systematically murdered by the Nazi regime in the name of diligent ethnic cleansing.

Edith Stein was passionate, purposeful, faithful, and committed. She was a brilliant philosopher who lived and thrived in the intellectual university community of 1910s Germany. She was also a young Jewish woman who shocked her intellectual community when she fell in love with Jesus Christ and became a Roman Catholic, being baptized in 1922. More shocking still, eleven years later, Edith entered the cloistered Carmelite order in Cologne, Germany, to follow a life of mystic and contemplative prayer in the cloister under the name Teresa Benedicta of the Cross. Today, as the meaning of feminism is lost in a world of relativism, Edith Stein provides a model for a true feminist—a woman who authentically integrates faith, family, and work.

In 1942, Edith and her sister Rosa, a lay Carmelite living with her at the monastery in Echt, Holland, were forcefully taken by the Gestapo and transported by train to the Auschwitz concentration camp, where they were both murdered in the gas chamber on August 9. Edith Stein's profound spirituality, however, had left a mark not only on those who had personally known her as a philosopher, a teacher, and a speaker, but also on all who learned of her through her many writings, essays, articles, letters, and stories.

"Today we live again in a time that urgently needs to be renewed at the hidden springs of God-fearing souls," Edith wrote for the feast of the Epiphany, 1941, a meditation requested by the Echt Prioress. "Many people, too, place their last hope in these hidden springs of salvation. This is a serious warning cry: Surrender without reservation to the Lord who has called us. This is required of us so that the face of the earth may be renewed. In faithful trust, we must abandon our souls to the sovereignty of the Holy Spirit.... We may live in confident certainty that what the Spirit of God secretly effects in us bears fruits in the kingdom of God. We will see them in eternity."

Not in spite of, but *because of*, Edith's hidden life, one can easily paraphrase what G. K. Chesterton wrote of Thomas More: if there had not been that particular woman at that particular moment, the whole of history would have been different. Not only is Edith Stein the first recognized saint in the Catholic Church since the end of the apostolic age to have been born and raised in a practicing Jewish family, but, even more significant, because of her legacy of faith and philosophy, our understanding of Catholicism is richer, deeper, and more profound.

Much like the spread of the Christian message in the early Church, the story of the Discalced Carmelite nun named Teresa Benedicta of the Cross, Edith Stein, traveled swiftly by word of mouth. And through ordeals that sound like an episode of *Mission Impossible*, Edith's original manuscripts were stashed away, concealed, and even literally buried underground during the Second World War, in an effort to preserve her unique and insightful work from the Nazi death machine. It is amazing and outright miraculous that so much of Edith's work was ultimately preserved—in spite of the gruesome persecution and physical devastation left behind by the war.

It is not hard to see, therefore, how the story of such a radical and orthodox Catholic woman could not only grab the attention of the community of believers, but also inspire them to follow the way to Christ. A short twenty years after her death, the official process of beatification and canonization for Edith Stein was set in motion. Whether through reading her numerous writings, which are now translated into several languages, or through hearing her story, it became natural to anticipate that Edith would one day be formally honored because of her faith. On May 1, 1987, she was beatified in Cologne by Pope John Paul II, in a ceremony attended by seventy thousand people, including some of her Jewish relatives and Carmelite Sisters who had known and lived with her.

Eleven years later (the same number of years that Edith waited between her baptism and her entry into Carmel) Edith Stein—the philosopher, convert to the Catholic Faith, Carmelite nun, and martyr at Auschwitz—was declared a saint in the Catholic Church. At a Mass in St. Peter's Square on Sunday, October 11, 1998, Pope John Paul II presented "this eminent daughter of Israel and faithful daughter of the Church as a saint to the whole world." At the liturgy attended by nearly one hundred members of the Stein family, many who remain devout Jews, the Holy Father declared, "The spiritual experience of Edith Stein is an eloquent example of this extraordinary interior renewal. A young woman in search of the truth has become a saint and martyr through the silent workings of divine grace: Teresa Benedicta of the Cross, who from heaven repeats to us today all the words that marked her life: Far be it from me to glory except in the Cross of our Lord Jesus Christ,'" the Pope continued, echoing the words of St. Paul to the Galatians (6:14).

Edith Stein died a follower of Jesus Christ, "offering her martyrdom for her fellow Jews," wrote Priors General Father Camilo Maccise, O.C.D., and Father Joseph Chalmers, O.Carm., in 1998 in a circular to Carmelite men and women around the world on the occasion of Edith Stein's canonization. "The canonization

Edith Stein: St. Teresa Benedicta of the Cross

of Edith Stein is a new plea that God makes to the Church, to Carmelites in particular, on the eve of the Third Millennium. The life of this great Jewish woman, who sought the truth and followed Jesus, offers a timely message for relations between faith and science, for ecumenical dialogue, for consecrated life and for spirituality, speaking, as it does, to the members of the Church and those outside it."[2]

This book honors the life of our Jewish sister, Sister Teresa Benedicta of the Cross, a martyr for her faith and for her Christ. It is not meant to be a definitive biography; rather, it is to be an introduction to Edith Stein and her life. Even as we continue the process of "getting to know" Edith, as more of her theological works, letters, and philosophical essays are translated into English, it is my hope that we never lose sight of the loving teacher and friend Edith Stein, who is still remembered by many of her students and colleagues in Europe. I echo the words of Carmelite Sister Josephine Koeppel, who recommended in a published interview: "Get to know her as a person with a heart that really can be touched. First, get to know her as that. *Then* respect her brilliance."

Ultimately, it is my hope and my prayer that you be inspired not simply by this holy woman's death but by her remarkable and heroic life. "Pure spirits are like rays of light through which the eternal light communes with creation," Edith once said. "To believe in saints, means only to sense in them God's presence."[3]

[2] Priors General Father Camilo Maccise, O.C.D., and Father Joseph Chalmers, O.Carm., "Losing to Win: The Journey of Bl. Teresa Benedicta of the Cross," August 9, 1998, http://www.helpfellowship.org/Edith/Edith_Stein_1998.htm.

[3] Susanne Batzdorff, trans. *An Edith Stein Daybook: To Live at the Hand of the Lord* (Springfield, IL: Templegate, 1994), 96, 106.

Carmelite Prayer

Lord, God of our ancestors, You brought St. Teresa Benedicta to the fullness of the science of the Cross at the hour of her martyrdom. Fill us with that same knowledge; and, through her intercession, allow us always to seek after You, the supreme Truth; and to remain faithful until death to the covenant of love ratified in the blood of Your Son for the salvation of all. Grant this through Christ our Lord. Amen.

Part 2

Life in a Jewish Family

Chapter 2

⌒

The Stein Family

The heroic life of Edith Stein began on October 12, 1891, in Breslau, Silesia (which was then mostly in Germany). A lovely medieval city of culture and religion, Breslau became Wroclaw when it
was ceded to Poland at the end of the Second World War. Edith,
the youngest of seven surviving children out of eleven, was born
on the feast day of Yom Kippur—the Day of Atonement—the
holiest day of the Jewish year, a fast day spent mostly in prayer.

For Edith, being born on Yom Kippur was more than a coincidence; it marked her destiny and proclaimed her lifelong desire
to find Truth. Yom Kippur, celebrated on the tenth of the Jewish
month of Tishri (September-October), is an opportunity for the
Jewish people each year to begin life anew, to return to God, and
to renew fidelity to Him. As Edith explains in *Life in a Jewish
Family*, "I was born on the Day of Atonement, and my mother
always considered it my real birthday, although celebrations and
gifts were always forthcoming on October 12. (She herself celebrated her birthday, according to the Jewish calendar, on the
Feast of Tabernacles; but she no longer insisted on this custom for
her children.)" And Edith, the child born as her mother, Auguste
Stein, observed Yom Kippur, was seen as a unique blessing by

Frau Stein. "She laid great stress on my being born on the Day of Atonement, and I believe this contributed more than anything else to her youngest's being especially dear to her."[4]

In her family's history, Edith meticulously recalls the life story of her mother, Auguste née Courant, and her ancestors. Of her father, Siegfried, however, Edith has no memories and few stories. When Edith was not yet two years old, her father died suddenly while he was away on a business trip, apparently of heat stroke.

> On a hot July day, he went to inspect a forest and had a long way to go on foot. From a distance, a postman going through that part of the countryside noticed him lying down but assumed he was simply resting and paid no more attention. Only when, several hours later, he returned by the same route and saw him still at the same spot did the man investigate and find him dead. My mother was informed, and she went to bring the body to Breslau. The place where my father died lies between Frauenwaldau and Goschütz. Close by, there is a sawmill where often the freshly felled trees were cut up into logs for us. The kindly people at this mill were a real support for my mother in those difficult days, and she never forgot them.... The friendship which developed thus was to last a lifetime." (*Life*, 41)

Siegfried Stein met Auguste Courant when she was only nine years old. "The earliest letter he wrote her is from that time,"

---

[4] Edith Stein, *Life in a Jewish Family: Her Unfinished Autobiographical Account*, ed. L. Gelber and Romaeus Leuven, O.C.D., trans. Josephine Koeppel, O.C.D. (Washington, DC: ICS Publications, 1986), 72.

Edith wrote in *Life in a Jewish Family*. "He and his sisters kept the correspondence going. In the letters of later years there gradually appeared references which showed how much they wished for an engagement" (ibid., 38). Siegfried was twenty-eight years old and Auguste twenty-one on their wedding day. They spent the first ten years of their life together in Gleiwitz, where Siegfried ran a lumber business with his mother. After their first six children were born, the family moved in 1881 from Gleiwitz to Lublinitz, where Siegfried established his own business. Nine years and four children later, Siegfried and Auguste moved to Breslau, hoping for better economic opportunities and better schools in the big city.

Edith, the youngest, was the only one of their children born in Breslau, in a residence on Kohlenstrasse, a place Edith describes as a "small apartment," which was torn down long before Edith began writing her family's story. "A lot was rented in the immediate neighborhood so the lumber business could be started anew.... Feeding the family became a real problem; the new business, burdened with debts, took a long time in getting on its feet," Edith wrote years later. "My mother never said a word about [any] difficulties she had in her marriage. She has always spoken of my father with a warm loving tone in her voice; even now, after so many decades, when she visits his grave, one can see she still grieves for him" (ibid., 41).

Some of Edith's brothers and sisters were literally adults when Edith was born. Auguste Courant Stein used to divide her family into three groups: the boys, the girls, and the children — the last two being "afterthoughts." Edith and her sister Erna, who was only eighteen months older, were bound from the beginning with a special friendship that lasted throughout their entire life. Although very different physically and in temperament, "we were inseparable," wrote Edith. "The older sisters used to say she was as transparent as clear water while they called me a book sealed with seven seals" (ibid., 63).

Physically, Edith describes herself as a child: "I was small and frail, and despite all the care given me, always pale; I wore my blond hair (which only later darkened) usually loose or merely tied with a ribbon" (ibid., 62). Erna remembered, "We were just [about] two years apart, and so it was a matter of course that, from our earliest childhood until we went our separate ways, we were very close, closer than any of our other brothers and sisters" (ibid., 14).

Erna noted in her own *Reminiscences*, written seven years after Edith's death, "[Edith's] earliest childhood coincided with the time when our mother experienced her greatest worries due to the sudden death of our father and when her work load was so great that she was unable to spend much time with us. We two 'little ones' were accustomed to get along together and to keep busy by ourselves, at least in the morning, before the older ones returned from school" (ibid., 14).

After her husband's death and against the advice of her own family, the forty-four-year-old widow took over the management of her husband's lumber business, a career field few women had entered.

> Our relatives came to my father's funeral and afterwards held a council on what my mother should do now with her seven children since she was without means: naturally she should sell the debt-ridden business; perhaps take a larger apartment and sublet furnished rooms. The brothers would contribute whatever was lacking. My mother remained silent the whole time, exchanging only a very

expressive look with her eldest daughter who was seventeen years old at the time. Her resolution had been made. She intended to cope by herself without accepting support from anyone.... She was a merchant's daughter and, by nature, possessed the special talents needed in business: her arithmetic was excellent; she had a gift for recognizing a business opportunity ... [and the] courage and decisiveness [to act].... Above all else, she was supremely gifted in dealing with people. She soon familiarized herself with the technical aspects and the special calculations made in the timber trade. (ibid., 42)

To everyone's surprise, the business prospered. "Gradually, step by step, she succeeded in working her way up. Even just to provide adequate food and clothing for seven children was no simple matter. We never went hungry; but we did have to accustom ourselves to the utmost in simplicity and thrift; and this habit has never left us to this day" (ibid., 42). Frau Stein also succeeded in paying off all her deceased husband's debts—and then began plans for the children's education. Her older children helped the widow Stein in running the house, as well as in the running of the business, becoming quickly familiar with the customers and the business procedures.

Most of the people my mother dealt with were craftsmen. She knew each one's family history. She found it out, usually, when they wanted goods on credit or when they could not redeem the notes they had given. My mother repeatedly followed her kind heart in these cases; sometimes she even gave the "bad customers" some additional cash when they were in need. She was often cheated; and the business was plagued with heavy losses. Despite that, it prospered.... One day a woman who had for a long time been my mother's friend visited us and exclaimed: "I must tell you at once what I just overheard in the streetcar. A few men were talking about the lumber trade here in Breslau, and one of them said: 'Do you know who is the most capable merchant in the whole trade in town? Frau Stein!'" (ibid., 601)

"Summer and winter [my mother] rose very early in the morning to go to the lumberyard," Edith wrote about that period in her life. "For years both the apartment and the business locale were rented; and she had a great deal to suffer from mean landlords. The apartment in Kohlenstrasse in which I was born left me with but a single recollection, the earliest memory I have, in fact.... I can see myself standing before a big white door, drumming on it with clenched fists and screaming because my elder sister was on the other side, and I wanted to go to her. Nor do I recall more about our next home in Schiesswerderstrasse where also we had our first business site. On the other hand, I remember the apartment at Jägerstrasse 5 very clearly. That is where I celebrated my third birthday, and we lived there for many years" (ibid., 54).

Frau Stein was a pious Jewish woman who instructed her children in Jewish traditions by her example, "a genuine Jewish mother," in Edith's words (ibid., 236). Among the "most important events of life at home, aside from the family feasts, were the major Jewish High Holy Days," Edith recalled later. "During my childhood, everything was done as prescribed; later, our liberal-minded elder brothers and sisters talked my mother out of some of it.... As things were, the celebrations lacked some of the solemnity due them since only my mother and the younger children participated with devotion. The brothers whose task it was, as substitute for their deceased father, to recite prayers, did so with little respect. When the elder one was absent and the younger had to represent the head of the house, he made clear his opinion that it was not to be taken seriously" (ibid., 68–70). Still, Auguste Stein persisted "with deep devotion, reciting the prescribed prayers." And the children, however secular, did not go to school on high holy days. Edith noted, "My mother does not usually go to the synagogue for the evening service but stays home, reciting the prescribed prayers from her prayer book" (ibid., 71).

When Edith was older, she became aware of just how efficiently Frau Stein was managing the business. "My mother always attributed this fact to being blessed by Heaven," Edith wrote years later. "On one occasion … she said to me, giving what she likewise considered a proof of God's existence: 'After all, I can't imagine that I owe everything I've achieved to my own ability.' This, of course, was correct" (ibid., 60). In spite of her older children's growing cynicism regarding their faith, Frau Stein continued to observe faithfully the Jewish holy days and make their children aware of God in their daily lives. Even her language, when speaking about future events, Edith remembered, always included the phrase "with the help of God" or "God willing" (ibid., 108).

"Edith's mother was devout; her faith in God was unshakable. She did what she could to instruct her family in her religion but she did not exact strict observance" from her children, wrote Sister Josephine Koeppel, O.C.D., the English translator of several of Edith's works. "One can see from Edith's own account that while they had no doubt about their mother's deep faith, the young Stein brothers and sisters seemed to take their Jewish religion rather more for granted than as a serious personal commitment" (ibid., 441). Even as she followed in her older siblings' footsteps and distanced herself from the faith of their mother, Edith never forgot that she had been born on the Day of Atonement.

For the Day of Atonement, the highest of all the Jewish festivals, "not only did my mother attend on this evening but she was accompanied by our elder sisters; even my brothers considered it a duty to be present. The beautiful ancient melodies used on this evening even attract those of other beliefs," Edith wrote in her family's biography. "From my thirteenth year ... I observed [Yom Kippur's] fast even when we no longer shared our mother's faith nor continued observing any of the ritual prescriptions when away from home" (ibid., 71–72).

Like most widows of her culture, Auguste Stein always wore black and, at home, an apron. She was known for her love of neighbor, a virtue that Edith, too, inherited. "To this day," Edith recalled about her mother's hobby of growing fruits and vegetables, "my mother is happiest when she is able to do her own sowing and [harvesting] and can give generously to others from the harvest. Doing so she follows faithfully the old Jewish custom that, instead of keeping for oneself the first of each kind of produce one rather gives them away" (ibid., 40).

As a child, Edith was no paragon of virtue. She was spoiled and was known to fly into a rage if not given what she wanted or if not the center of attention.[5] "I went through sudden transitions, incomprehensible to the observer," Edith wrote.

> During my early years, I was mercurially lively, always in motion, spilling over with pranks, impertinent and precocious, and, at the same time, intractably stubborn

[5] See Ruth Miriam Irey, O.C.D. "Sister Benedicta of the Cross (Edith Stein): Her Faith, Her Philosophy, Her People" (unpublished essay, 1998), 2.

and angry if anything went against my will. My eldest
sister, whom I loved very much, tested her newly-acquired
child-training methods on me in vain. Her last resort was
to lock me in a dark room. When this danger loomed, I
would lie on the floor, stiff with resistance; and it took
superhuman effort for my frail sister to lift me and carry
me off. In my dark prison, in no way resigned to my fate,
instead, screaming at the top of my lungs, I hammered
on the door with both fists until my mother would finally
declare we were exceeding the limit of tolerance to be
expected of the other tenants; she then set me free. (ibid.,
73–74)

Even as a young child, Edith wrote in *Life in a Jewish Family*,
she had within her "a hidden world" that reveals her spiritual
sensitivity:

Whatever I saw or heard throughout my days was pon-
dered over there. The sight of a drunkard could haunt
and plague me for days and nights on end. Later, I was
often grateful that as far as my brothers were concerned
there was never any danger of their being intoxicated,
nor had I ever to see any near relative in such a disgusting condition. I could never understand how one could
possibly laugh at such a state; and in my student years ...
I began to abstain from even a drop of alcohol to avoid
being personally responsible for losing even the smallest
particle of my freedom and spirit and my human dignity.
Should anyone speak of a murder in my presence, I would
lie awake for hours that night, and, in the dark, horror
would press in upon me from every corner. Indeed, even
a somewhat coarse expression which, in irritation, my

mother once used in my presence, pained me so deeply that I could never forget this minor incident, an argument with my eldest brother. (ibid., 74)

In what would later become Edith's trademark silence about her innermost self, she wrote of this "hidden world" and its effect on her: "I never mentioned a word to anyone of these things which caused me so much hidden suffering. It never occurred to me that one could speak about such matters. Only infrequently did I give my family any inkling of what was happening: for no apparent reason I sometimes developed a fever and in delirium spoke of the things which were oppressing me inwardly.... It is easy to surmise that such sudden outbursts alarmed my relatives. They called it 'nerves' and tried, as much as possible, to shield me from overexcitement" (ibid., 74–75).

From her sister Erna's point of view, "as far as I know from my Mother's stories and those of my siblings, and according to my own recollections, we were fairly well-behaved and rarely quarreled. One of my earliest memories is that Paul, my oldest brother, carried Edith around the room and sang student songs to her, or that he showed her the illustrations in a history of literature and lectured her on Schiller, Goethe, etc. She had an excellent memory and retained everything. Many of our numerous uncles and aunts would tease or try to confuse her by telling her that *Maria Stuart* was written by Goethe, or the like. This misfired with deadly certainty" (ibid., 14).

When Erna started school, Edith, who was accustomed to keeping up with everything her older "twin" did, rebelled against the idea that she could attend only kindergarten. For her birthday in October that year, she asked for only one birthday present: to be admitted late into school when she turned six years old. Through her big sister Else's intervention, Edith was granted her wish, on probation. "But by the following Easter [when the school year began], I was promoted with the others; and from that time on I always maintained my place among the best students" (ibid., 78).

In Erna's words:

> From the fourth or fifth year, she began to show some knowledge of literature. When I started school, she felt terribly alone. Therefore Mother decided to send her to kindergarten. That was a complete fiasco. She felt so dreadfully unhappy there and was intellectually so far ahead of the other children that they gave up on that, also. Very soon after that she began to plead to be allowed to start school that autumn, since she would be six years old on October 12. And, although she was exceptionally small and no one believed her to be six, the principal of Victoria School in Breslau was willing to grant her urgent request; we four older sisters had been attending that school before her. So she began her schooling on her sixth birthday, October 12, 1897. Since it was not the custom at that time to start the school year in autumn, Edith attended the lowest grade for six months only. Despite that, she was one of the top students by Christmas. She was gifted as well as diligent, dependable, and possessed of great perseverance. However, she was never inordinately ambitious in a bad sense; instead she was a good comrade, ever ready to be of help." (ibid., 15)

When Edith was about seven years old, she experienced what she labeled as her "first great transformation." Much like her eventual conversion or, for that matter, any of the life-changing decisions she was to make later, this transformation in Edith was immediate, decisive, and permanent. "I would not be able to ascribe it to any external cause. I cannot explain it otherwise than that reason assumed command within me," she wrote in *Life in a Jewish Family*. "I recall very well how, from that time on, I was convinced that my mother and my sister Frieda had better knowledge of what was good for me than I had; and because of this confidence, I readily obeyed them. The old stubbornness seemed to disappear; and, in the years that followed, I was a docile child. When I did permit myself some naughtiness or an impudent answer, I quickly sought forgiveness although the effort to bring myself to do so cost me a great deal; but, afterwards, I was very happy to have peace restored" (ibid., 75).

Even in the moments when temptation got the best of her, Edith remained even-keeled. "Angry outbursts became all but non-existent; early in life I arrived at such a degree of self-mastery that I could preserve my equanimity almost without a struggle. I do not know how that happened; I do believe what cured me was the distaste and shame I experienced at the angry outbursts of others and the acute realization I had that the price of such self-indulgence was the loss of one's dignity" (ibid., 75).

And so, with the same passion and obsession that she had expressed her outbursts earlier in life, at the end of reason, Edith was transformed. Gradually, she recalled later, her "inner world grew lighter and clearer. Whatever was heard, seen, read, or experienced offered my active fantasy material for the most intrepid constructions." Edith's creative soul and "lively spirit" merged. "In my dreams I always foresaw a brilliant future for myself. I dreamed about happiness and fame, for I was convinced that I was destined for something great and that I did not belong at all in the narrow, bourgeois circumstances into which I had been born. About these dreams I said as little as I had about the fears which had plagued me earlier. However, that I was given to daydreaming was apparent; and when anyone noticed that I was oblivious to what was going on, they would startle me out of my reverie. With such a prolific fantasy," Edith summarized, "it was a good thing that I got to go to school early so that my lively spirit received solid nourishment" (ibid., 77).

Edith manifested from the beginning extraordinary intellectual gifts and a zest for learning. Her determination and resolve made her an excellent student who always desired to be first in her class.

> As a pupil I was overly zealous. I was apt to skip right to the front of the teacher's desk with index finger raised in order to "get my turn." ... At the beginning of each new school year, I greedily devoured the new textbooks for literature and history. The first thing in the morning, I would begin to read while my mother fixed my hair. I loved to write compositions; they enabled me to include some of the thoughts which occupied my mind.... When not in school, I became so quiet and taciturn that the whole family noticed it. This was probably due to my being so cocooned in my interior world. Perhaps it was also because of the condescending way most adults deal with children.... Consequently, I preferred to keep quiet. I was taken seriously in school. (ibid., 79)

Edith also enjoyed and often created skits, playlets, and poems for special occasions, a tradition she continued into adulthood, including writing poems for her mother's birthdays that she had the grandchildren recite.

Edith was also an exceptional Latin scholar. Long before she prayed in Latin or thought of it as the language of the Church,

Edith Stein: St. Teresa Benedicta of the Cross

notes Patricia Hampl in her essay "A Book Sealed with Seven Seals: Edith Stein," when she seeks to express the indescribable, when "her passion quickens at the edge of the inexpressible, she resorts instinctively to Latin and its crisp, minimalist beauty.... Just as the precision of Bach and his elegant resolution of great complexities made him her favorite composer, so it was that of all her languages (and she was a gifted linguist, easily adding Greek and English, French and Dutch, as she went through life), Latin was the tongue that best suited her."[6] Edith described it this way: "Latin was something else again; far more enjoyable even than studying modern languages, this grammar with its strict rules fascinated me. It was as though I were learning my mother tongue. That it was the language of the Church and that later I should pray in this language never even occurred to me at the time" (ibid., 156).

[6] Patricia Hampl, *I Could Tell You Stories: Sojourns in the Land of Memory* (New York: W. W. Norton, 1999), 119, 120.

Chapter 3

German Jews: A Brief Historical Setting

In order to understand the life of the Jewish family—the type described by Edith in her family's biography—as well as the point of view of the Steins toward Edith's choices and to the world events that later unfolded and engulfed them, it is critical to have at least a background historical understanding of the German Jews.

The Jewish presence in Germany goes back to the fall of Jerusalem in A.D. 70, when the Roman troops destroyed the city and dispersed its population—sending a wave of Jews into Diaspora living. The Roman victory, noted Ruth Gay in *The Jews of Germany: A Historical Portrait*, coincided with the planting of a new Roman colony on the Rhine, which the Germans later called Köln (Cologne). "Cologne, the new colony, was a promising stopping place for the Jewish exiles, then essentially an agricultural people. By the third century, some Jews had become significant wine growers while others had established themselves as merchants, artisans, or doctors. Some may even have served in the Roman legions."[7]

[7] Ruth Gay, *The Jews of Germany: A Historical Portrait* (New Haven, CT: Yale University Press, 1992), 4.

Edith Stein: St. Teresa Benedicta of the Cross

Centuries later, in 1012, the chronicles of Cologne note that the Jewish community built a synagogue. Historical records present a picture of Jews living as an identifiable group in many of the communities along the Rhine. "In these early centuries of Christian rule, as the pagan Roman order and pagan hegemony gave way to the church, the Jews emerged as only one of many people — Romans, Franks, Lombards, Saxons, Bavarians, Thuringians — making up the Holy Roman Empire," even enjoying certain favors under individual Roman rulers. Many centuries passed, in fact, "before Jews came to be treated as outcasts in a Christian world" (Gay, *Jews of Germany*, 6).

Jewish communities along the Rhine enjoyed a pattern of "privilege, protection, and intercession" by their overlords. "But as a distinct community, the Jews of Ashkenaz (the Hebrew term for Germany) were only at the beginning of their extraordinary odyssey. In Ashkenaz they created a new language, a new culture, and a new center for Jewish life" (ibid., 9).

The Crusades, however, marked the end of the Jews as a "recognized if distinct element in the cultures in which they lived," becoming now the "marked men and women" of Europe. In spite of the fact that the Jews living in established communities were defended by the ruling bishops or took refuge with their Christian neighbors, the trek of the Crusaders through Ashkenaz as the Crusaders traveled to Jerusalem to reclaim the city from the Muslims left behind a great slaughter of Jews, "an omen of the cruel anti-Semitism of the next century" (ibid., 12).

In his discussion of Pope John Paul II's statements to the Jewish leaders of Cologne shortly before Edith Stein's beatification, Dr. Eugene J. Fisher noted the Pope's description of the "heroic testimony" of witness of the Jews of the Rhineland during this period. "'Heroic witness,' of course, is the precise meaning of the term 'martyrdom.' In the first part of this statement the pope is alluding, and not subtly, to the attempt at forced conversion and then massacre (when they refused) of the Jews of the Rhineland by marauding stragglers of the First Crusade in 1096, an attack opposed by the pope and the bishops of the time but one which took thousands of lives," explained Fisher, associate director of the U.S. Bishops' Office for Ecumenical and Interreligious Affairs. "The pope here sees the Christians who perpetrated the event as the evildoers they were and acknowledges their Jewish victims as martyrs for the true faith given by God to Israel."[8]

Sporadic horrors, born from the Crusades, were visited upon the German Jews; but it was the thirteenth century that permanently and systematically transformed the Jewish circumstances in Germany. "It was not until the thirteenth century that the parallel existence of Jew and Christian suddenly became charged with the fury that would poison Jewish existence. In a single century, distinctive Jewish dress was introduced, the blood libel was invented, and Jews were first depicted as Satanic figures. In the German lands alone a particularly disgusting portrait emerged: the Jew as the familiar of the pig. As Christians were aware, Jews felt a special repugnance toward pigs, whose flesh was forbidden food. Linking the two therefore had a particular appeal for malevolent caricaturists in Germany" (Gay, *Jews of Germany*, 23).

In her book *Aunt Edith*, Edith's niece Susanne Batzdorff relates an anti-Semitic incident in the history of the Jewish community in Breslau—one that still haunted the community and her family centuries later. The fact that it was still retold with

---

[8] Susanne Batzdorff, *Aunt Edith: The Jewish Heritage of a Catholic Saint* (Springfield, IL: Templegate, 1998), 15.

such passion by Edith's brother-in-law sheds some light on the depth and intensity of feeling with which Edith's family would have experienced the news of her baptism and later entrance into Carmel. In 1453, Batzdorff recalled, the Jews of Breslau were driven out of the city—and forty-one Jews were burned at the stake—after Franciscan friar John of Capistrano accused them of desecrating the Host. "My father would remark that, whenever he crossed the Blücherplatz (now Solny pl.) he could smell the stench of acrid smoke from the burning flesh of his fellow-Jews centuries before," Batzdorff wrote. "In fact, in his last long talk with his sister-in-law Edith Stein, Father used his most persuasive arguments to try to turn her away from her plan to become a Carmelite, and this was one of the arguments he brought to bear in his efforts" (*Aunt Edith*, 36).

By the Middle Ages, Edith's birth-city of Breslau ranked among the larger cities of the German Empire, a center of trade with as many as fifteen thousand inhabitants. The River Oder, which figures prominently in Edith's family history, was critical to the city's development (see *Life*, 447). By 1530, throughout Germany, a yellow badge for Jews was required on their coat or cap "so that they may be recognized," as proclaimed by the Imperial Police Code (see Gay, *Jews of Germany*, 22–23). Throughout the Middle Ages, in fact, Jews in Europe were often thrown out or run out of various cities by attacks, blamed as the cause for everything from individual rulers' misguided policies to the Black Death plague.

The position in society of German Jews by the seventeenth century was that of "unequal 'partners' in a transaction in which a ruler provided them with a place to live and work, and the Jews in return paid protection money—*Schutzgeld*—for the privilege of existence. In those years, both Jews and their rulers saw themselves engaged in an exchange of services, unclouded by philosophic considerations." Ideas such as "toleration, human rights, and mutual moral obligations" were not part of this clearly defined business transaction (ibid., 90). By 1776, there were nearly two thousand Jews living in Breslau.

Pressures for change in the Jewish place in society, however, began to build, both within and outside the Jewish community. By the time the nineteenth century began, everything pointed toward liberation and integration—perceived by the Jewish community as its emancipation. Although acculturation or secularization of the Jews was not universal throughout Germany, "communal organization, the ceremony of circumcision, secular education, the prevalence of Yiddish—indeed, the very survival of Judaism as a religion—were put into question." Education became the central issue for German Jews, seen as the key for them to fit in into what was clearly "a new age.... By the beginning of the nineteenth century, Jewish parents had a variety of alternatives. Some local governments invited or even required Jewish children to attend state schools. Church-sponsored and nondenominational schools also made room for Jewish children" (ibid., 120, 118).

Politically, Jewish emancipation in the German lands was a process rather than an event. Because of its design as a conglomeration of some three hundred states of various sizes and rulers, what later became Imperial Germany dealt with the "Jewish question" in regional trends. "Privileges were granted and revoked. Anti-Semitic riots disputed in fact what had been declared in law, and the status of the Jews was one of the many pawns to be exchanged or moved in the aftermath of the wars and revolutions that punctuated the century." Jews, who throughout their history in the Diaspora had sought legal guarantees, saw a "glimpse of the

Promised Land" on March 11, 1812, when an edict on the Jews was proclaimed, "conferring on them the right to full citizenship, the right to settle wherever they chose, the right to buy land (if they took German names), the right to serve in the army, and the right to marry freely (including non-Jews). It also removed all discriminatory taxes.... The edict of 1812 put the Jews at last on an equal legal footing with their fellow citizens. Although the rights in this edict were withdrawn piecemeal and in the end not renewed until 1871, the Jews' attitude toward their new position in the world was changing. They no longer were willing to live on sufferance but fought for every social, economic, and cultural advance as a matter of right" (ibid., 131, 127).

The springtime of national identity, which took place in 1848 across the European continent, is a critical element in understanding the Jewish community into which Edith Stein was born. It was then that the principles that define a nation confronted each other: Is a nation a community bound together by residence within a given territory? Or is a nation a community bound together by ties of language, tradition, and religion, or culture in general? By the late 1800s in Germany, nationalism as an allegiance to an ethnic kin became the dominant motive force. Jews, however, "felt themselves as Germans," noted Susanne Batzdorff, "and saw their fate intertwined with that of the country in which they lived and which had already bestowed citizenship on them in 1812" (*Aunt Edith*, 42). As Edith tells us in *Life in a Jewish Family*, her mother found inconceivable the notion that she was not German.

And yet reality was otherwise. "During the fifty years of the German monarchy, Jews could not become officers and were rarely appointed to teaching positions or higher positions of public office. The social segregation of the Jews was still in evidence.

At the university, the fraternities excluded Jews from membership" (ibid., 43).

On April 20, 1889, Adolf (Adi) Hitler was born in neighboring Braunau am Inn, Austria—only two years before Edith Stein was born.

Chapter 4

~

Edith's Changing World

Novelist Jakob Wassermann was born two years after the Franco-Prussian War, which ended in 1871, the year of "Jewish Emancipation." While he agonized over the question of Jewish assimilation, Wassermann's thoughts offer an illustration of the world of German Jews into which Edith was born less than two decades later. "[After 1871] the day of civic rights had long since dawned for the German Jews. . . . I remember that on various occasions my father would say with happy satisfaction, `We live in the age of tolerance!' . . . In dress, speech and style of life, the acculturation (of the Jews) was in every way complete. The school I attended was state-supported and public. We lived among Christians, socialized with Christians and for progressive Jews, such as my father, there was a Jewish community only in the sense of religious ceremonies and traditions. And these ceremonies shrank back more and more, because of the temptations and the powerful forces of modernity, into secretive, alienated and desperate sects. Traditions became matters of legend, finally only words and an empty shell" (Gay, *Jews of Germany*, 185).

Scholar Paul Mendes-Flohr, however, presented the circumstances of German Jews with a different light. While German

Jews assimilated the cultural values of Germany, they were not assimilated into German society. "They remained by and large socially apart; hence, their assimilation was never as complete or absolute as is commonly believed. Assimilation — 'acculturation' is undoubtedly a better term — was a highly differentiated process in which Jewish identity, knowledge, and commitment were maintained in varying degrees. Acculturation thus cannot be facilely equated with an abandonment of Judaism."[9] German Jews at the turn of the century entered the universities in numbers that Mendes-Flohr described as "disproportionate to their representation in the population of Germany and elsewhere in Central Europe." This "energetic entrance" of Jews into "the educated bourgeoisie" of Central Europe "led to a spectacular flowering of Jewish creativity" (Mendes-Flohr, *German Jews*, 30). Noting Jewish women, in particular, "it has been estimated that in 1901 in all of Germany the percentage of Jewish women enrolled in gymnasia was 42, compared to only 4 percent of gentile women.... In Prussia in 1901, when women were finally permitted to take the Abitur examinations, which qualify those who pass for university study, the first contingent of fifty-six women included seventeen Jews, or 30 percent of the total" (ibid., 33).

While acknowledging that on the eve of the Nazi takeover "the German-Jewish community had undergone quantitative diminution through modernization, logical fragmentation, low fertility or conversion," historian Peter Pulzer remarked that what is noteworthy is the "degree of cohesion that the Jews of Germany retained. It was remarkable, given all these forces that tended to diminish the strength of Jewish identity, not that one Jew in

[9] Paul Mendes-Flohr, *German Jews: A Dual Identity* (New Haven, CT: Yale University Press, 1999), 3.

four should marry 'out,' but that three in four should continue to marry 'in.' What we have to explain, therefore, is the survival, in many respects the very vigorous survival, of Germany's Jews as a group until the politically-inspired assault on their existence under the Third Reich."[10]

German Jews found "a substitute in secular organizations for a civic structure that was decreasingly based on the synagogue. The *Centralverein*, founded in 1893, had a membership of forty thousand by 1914 and sixty thousand by 1932, which suggests that it represented between one-third and one-half of Jewish families. The Jewish women's organization, the *Jüdischer Frauenbund*, founded in 1904, had thirty-two thousand members in 1913 and some fifty thousand in the 1920s. Youth, student, and sporting organizations flourished to an equal extent. Some of these had a specific program—Zionist or Orthodox—but the majority were concerned with representing Jewish interests and maintaining a Jewish identity within general society. They were open equally to the religiously observant and nonobservant. The effect of this was felt externally as well as internally. The new organizations 'provided new ways of being Jewish'; they also maintained, and indeed increased, the visibility of Jews as a group, not merely as individuals" (Pulzer, *Jews and the German State*, 13).

Edith's hometown of Breslau was the capital of Silesia and a long-established site of a populous and active Jewish community. The city is equidistant from the borders that, in her time, marked Poland and Bohemia. German was the language and culture of this city of four hundred thousand inhabitants, home to the third largest Jewish community in Germany. "With its sparkling rivers,

[10] Peter Pulzer, *Jews and the German State: The Political History of a Minority, 1848–1933* (Oxford: Blackwell, 1992), 7.

picturesque islands, verdant parks and attractive suburbs, Breslau was a city where one enjoyed beautiful walks and hikes through the countryside by taking almost any trolley to the end of the line and setting out on foot from there. A level, wooded path alongside the Oder River was a favorite weekend destination. There families walked with small children, enjoyed the peaceful rural environment just a short distance from the noise and traffic of the city and perhaps ended their walk at the *Oderschlösschen* (little castle by the Oder) and delighted in a light refreshment" (Batzdorff, *Aunt Edith*, 31).

The Jews of this area "were in large part descended from the merchant Jews of the early Middle Ages who joined migrants from Central Europe and took refuge in Bohemia and Poland during the years of the Crusades. The new communities formed showed the cultural superiority of the Western Jew who spoke the language of their adopted country.... Their skills and creative talents contributed to the welfare of their newly adopted land. This usually won them the appreciation of the indigenous peoples, but, in too many cases, resentment and envy as well" (*Life*, 447).

Breslau was also an important cultural center. And Edith loved to participate in its offerings. She remembered years later:

> Every time the presentation of a classical drama was announced, it was as though I had been tendered a personal invitation. An anticipated evening at the theater was like a brilliant star which gradually drew nearer. I counted the intervening days and hours. It was a great delight just to sit in the theater and wait for the heavy iron curtain to be raised slowly; the call bell finally sounded; and the new unknown world was revealed. Then I became

totally immersed in the happenings on the stage, and the humdrum of everyday disappeared. I loved the classical operas as much as I did the great tragedies. The first I heard was *The Magic Flute*. We bought the piano score and soon knew it by heart. So, too, with *Fidelio*, which always remained my favorite. I also heard Wagner and during a performance found it impossible wholly to evade its magic. Still I repudiated this music, with the sole exception of *Die Meistersinger*. I had a predilection for Bach. This world of purity and strict regularity attracted me most intimately. Later when I came to know Gregorian chant, I felt completely at home for the first time; and then I understood what had moved me so much in Bach. (ibid., 171–172)

Frau Stein bought a lumberyard at Matthiasstrasse 151 in 1903. Seven years later, the family moved into a large house close by, where Edith spent her last years in high school. The spacious house, which they called "the Villa," is located at 38 Michaelisstrasse, now ul. Nowowiejska 38.

My grandmother, Auguste Stein, acquired this house about 1910 [recalled Erna's daughter Susanne Batzdorff in an article tracing her return to Breslau in 1995]. Both my brother and I were born here. We lived in this house until September 1933. Edith Stein spent her vacations here, and from here she left to become a Carmelite in October 1933. Grandmother Stein died here in 1936. When the Government declared that Jews could no longer own real estate, the house had to be sold to an Aryan—at a much reduced price, of course.... For us this house holds within its now decrepit walls and drab shell the memory of a large, vibrant family that once lived there under one roof in a time of peace and relative tranquility almost unimaginable today. In its large living room, birthdays and Passover Seder were celebrated. On its ground floor, my mother had her medical practice. In fact, in the exact place where Mother's medical shingle used to hang, right next to the front door, there is now a memorial plaque to Edith Stein in Polish, German and Hebrew.[11]

That the house is now owned by the Edith Stein Society of Wroclaw and dedicated to the cause of Catholic-Jewish dialogue and to building improved relations between Germans and Poles is a "comfort" to Edith's niece. "In a way, it is a development which has been brought about despite the horrors of the Holocaust and of war, but also because of them. I shall not speculate what Auguste Stein or her daughter Edith might think of this, but for us, the survivors, it appears somehow appropriate" (Batzdorff, *Aunt Edith*, 87–88).

With the same resolve with which Edith had forced her way into starting school a year before she was supposed to, she decided in 1906, at the age of fifteen, that she wanted a break from school. To her family's astonishment, Edith simply announced that she wanted to quit. "In no way would my mother oppose my categorical decision," Edith wrote of her mother's response. " 'I won't coerce you,' she said. 'I allowed you to start school when you wanted to go. By the same token, you may now leave if that is what you want.' So I quit school and, a few weeks later, traveled to Hamburg" (*Life*, 139).

<hr/>

[11] Susanne Batzdorff, "Tracing Edith Stein's Past," *America* (November 25, 1995): 12–17.

Edith's Changing World

Erna Biberstein, her closest-in-age sister, remembered:

> Although [Edith] achieved excellent grades all through
> her years in school, and we all assumed as a matter of
> course that, once finished with her studies at the girls'
> school, Edith, like me, would take the new *Realgymnasium*
> at the [*Viktoria Schule*] in order to [qualify for admission
> to] the university, she surprised us all by her decision to
> leave school. Since she was still tiny and delicate, my
> mother agreed and sent Edith, at first, to my oldest sister
> Else, partly to get a rest and partly to help Else who was
> married, lived in Hamburg, and had three small children.
> Edith stayed there for eight months and carried out her
> duties conscientiously and tirelessly even though house-
> work did not suit her well. When my mother went to
> visit there after about six months, she hardly recognized
> Edith. She had grown a lot, had gained weight and looked
> radiant. (ibid., 15)

From May 1906 to March 1907, Edith lived with her sister
Else in Hamburg. It was there, away from her mother and her
extended family, that Edith resolved her personal "question" of
faith, choosing to renounce all belief. "My existence in Hamburg,
now that I look back on it, seems to me to have been like that
of a chrysalis in its cocoon," Edith wrote in her memoirs. "I was
restricted to a very tight circle and lived in a world of my own
even more exclusively than I had at home. I read as much as the
housework would permit me. I heard and also read much that
was not good for me. Because of my brother-in-law's [medical]
specialization, some of the books that found their way into his
house were hardly intended for a fifteen-year-old girl. Besides,
Max and Else were totally without belief; religion had no place

whatsoever in their home." Yet her ethical idealism remained, as she believed that "we are in the world to serve humanity. Deliberately and consciously, I gave up praying here" (ibid., 148).

Edith's niece, however, points out that when Edith tells "that she lost her faith at the age of 15, we must keep in mind that it was not out of a thorough familiarity with Judaism." In an article, originally published in the *New York Times* just prior to her aunt's beatification, Batzdorff wrote, "It is intriguing, however futile, to speculate what might have happened to her spiritual development had she turned to a more intensive study of Judaism instead of Catholicism."[12] Ultimately, however, Batzdorff disagrees with most biographers and commentators who deduce from this statement that Edith Stein became an atheist at age fifteen. "I would submit that this gives too much weight to one brief remark," wrote Batzdorff in *Aunt Edith*. "First of all, Edith only tells us that she stopped praying. We do not know what sort of prayers she had been accustomed to until then.... Besides, a thoughtful young woman, who is searching for the truth, as Edith was fated to do all her life, is bound to struggle with doubts and uncertainties, especially during her teenage years. In the process of growing up, Edith was destined to experience a number of shifts in her thinking. That a fifteen-year-old does not pray is probably much more common than that she should observe this fact in herself and comment upon it" (*Aunt Edith*, 67).

Whether an avowed atheist, a temporarily agnostic searcher, or a teenager testing her freedom, Edith's time in Hamburg certainly changed and defined her. In a language that resembles Edith's own description of her first sudden and decisive

---

[12] Susanne Batzdorff, *Edith Stein: Selected Writings* (Springfield, IL: Templegate, 1990), 106.

"transformation" at the age of seven, Edith recalled later, "My decisions arose out of a depth that was unknown even to myself. Once a matter was bathed in the full light of consciousness and had acquired a definite form in my thoughts, I was no longer to be deterred by anything; indeed I found it an intriguing kind of sport to overcome hindrances which were apparently insurmountable" (*Life*, 152).

In 1908, nineteen-year-old Adolf Hitler applied to the Vienna Academy of Fine Arts—and was rejected for a second time, this time not even being admitted to take the entrance exam. That same year, in Breslau, seventeen-year-old Edith Stein decided to prepare on her own—and with the help of tutors—to make up the work she had missed in order to enter the *Obersekunda*, the equivalent of her eleventh year of high school. With the help of tutors in Latin and mathematics, Edith passed the entrance examination with flying colors.

"So I became a student again," Edith notes plainly. "Among the students in the class, there were seven other Jewish girls besides Julia and myself, but none of us received a strictly-orthodox upbringing" (ibid., 159–160). By their first reports that fall, Edith was already at the top of her class. From Easter 1908 until Easter 1911 she attended the *Realgymnasium* branch of *Viktoria Schule*, a municipal girls' school in Breslau. By passing a supplementary examination in Greek at *Johannesgymnasium*, the boys' school, along with the examination to graduate that was the norm, Edith earned a leaving certificate. Erna noted, "She was, as always, at the head of her class and at the finals, when she took her *Abitur*, she was excused from the oral examination." Aside from school, Erna wrote in her *Reminiscences* years later, "[Edith] participated fully in all our social activities; she was never a spoilsport. One could entrust to her all one's troubles and secrets; she was always ready to advise and to help and all confidences were in good hands with her" (ibid., 16).

Although Edith inherited a love of learning from her mother and her older siblings, only the two youngest Stein children, Edith and Erna, were able to study at the university. And the determination and persistence in learning so evident in Edith as a young child continued to manifest itself throughout her academic career, including her entrance to the University of Breslau, where she matriculated on April 28, 1911 — only three years after women were first admitted to academic education in Prussia.

Batzdorff describes the circle of university friends that her mother, Erna, and her aunt Edith shared, many of whom remained lifelong friends. "Somehow they drew other congenial students like a magnet, people who were thoughtful, intelligent, but who also had a sense of humor and found enjoyment in outdoor activities. They played tennis, hiked and climbed mountains. Most were not affluent and lived frugally. All were academically ambitious and politically aware. They adopted causes such as women's suffrage and various [types of] social legislation. Though they were patriotic Germans, they shied away from uncritical or fanatic nationalism, partly because such thinking often went hand in hand with anti-Semitism, and most of their friends were Jewish" (*Aunt Edith*, 106).

In Erna's own words, "The university years (I had begun to study medicine in 1909) were for us a time of serious study but also of wonderful sociability. We had a large circle of friends of both sexes with whom we spent our free time and our vacations in an atmosphere of freedom and lack of constraint which was unusual for that time. We discussed scientific and social topics in larger groups or in the more intimate circle of our friends.

Because of her unassailable logic and her wide knowledge in matters of literature and philosophy, Edith set the pace for us in these discussions. During our vacations, filled with a zest for living and adventure, we took trips to the mountains" (*Life*, 16).

Edith, however, "was indignant over the indifference with which most of the university students regarded current prob-lems," she wrote later in her memoirs. "Some of them were intent only on their own amusement during the early semesters while others were anxious only to get enough knowledge to meet the requirements of the examinations in order to feather their nests. My deep concern of social responsibility also made me decidedly favor women's suffrage.... The Prussian Society for Women's Right to Vote, which I joined with my women friends because it advocated full political equality for women, was made up mostly of socialists" (ibid., 191). With more than a grain of jest, Edith noted her own uncompromising attitude when discussing the issue of both husband and wife having independent careers. "We were all passionately moved by the women's rights movement.... We often discussed the issue of a double career. Erna and our two girl friends had many misgivings, wondering whether one ought not to give up a career for the sake of marriage. I was alone in maintaining always that I would not sacrifice my profession on any account. If one could have predicted the future for us then! The other three married but, nevertheless, continued in their careers. I alone did not marry, but I alone have assumed an obligation for which, joyfully, I would willingly sacrifice any other career," Edith added, hinting at her future in the Carmel (ibid., 123).

From Easter 1911 to Easter 1913, Edith studied philosophy, psychology, history, and German philology at the University of Breslau, enrolling in the Department of Experimental Psychology.

Edith Stein: St. Teresa Benedicta of the Cross

Although aspects of psychology intrigued and attracted her, it was a work in philosophy that she came across while studying for one of her classes that truly grabbed her attention. "In the essays I studied in preparation for these reviews, I kept coming across references to Edmund Husserl's *Logische Untersuchungen* [*Logical Investigations*]. One day Dr. [Georg] Moskiewicz [a friend] found me thus occupied in the psychology seminar. 'Leave all that stuff aside,' he said, 'and just read this; after all, it's where all the others got their ideas.' He handed me a thick book: the second Volume of Husserl's *Logische Untersuchungen*. I would have pounced on it at once but could not; my semester assignments would not permit it. But I determined to devote my next vacation to it. Mos knew Husserl personally; having studied with him for one semester in Göttingen, he always yearned to return there. 'In Göttingen that's all you do: philosophize, day and night, at meals, in the street, everywhere. All you talk about is "phenomena"'" (ibid., 217–218). At the same time, during this, her fourth semester in Breslau, "I got the impression that Breslau had no more to offer me and that I needed new challenges. Objectively, this was not at all correct," she acknowledged. "Plenty of unused opportunities were left, and here I would have been able to add a great deal to my knowledge. But I longed to go somewhere else" (ibid., 217).

Part 3

Edith the Philosopher

Chapter 5

⌒

"My Desire for Truth Was Itself a Prayer"

Teacher and Rabbi Abraham Heschel once said, "The most important things happen on the invisible side."

For Edith Stein, whose entire life was a quest for truth and meaning, her hidden world held the key to what was invisible to the eye — long before Truth had a name. Stein herself realized this after becoming a Christian. In a letter to a Benedictine nun friend, she said, "Whoever seeks the truth is seeking God, whether consciously or unconsciously." As Pope John Paul II remarked at Stein's canonization Mass, "Long before she realized it, she was caught by this fire" of the love of Christ. "At the beginning she devoted herself to freedom. For a long time Edith Stein was a seeker. Her mind never tired of searching and her heart always yearned for hope. She traveled the arduous path of philosophy with passionate enthusiasm. Eventually she was rewarded: she seized the truth. Or better: she was seized by it. Then she discovered that truth had a name: Jesus Christ. From that moment on, the incarnate Word was her One and All."

As the Pope noted, Edith Stein was able to understand that "the love of Christ and human freedom are intertwined, because love and truth have an intrinsic relationship. The quest for truth and its expression in love did not seem at odds to her; on the contrary she realized that they call for one another.... Truth and love need each other. St. Teresa Benedicta is a witness to this. The 'martyr for love,' who gave her life for her friends, let no one surpass her in love.... St. Teresa Benedicta of the Cross says to us all: Do not accept anything as truth if it lacks love. And do not accept anything as love which lacks truth! One without the other becomes a destructive life."

By all accounts, Edith Stein was a brilliant woman.

Edith was attracted to and studied under the philosophy of Edmund Husserl, the father of phenomenology—a philosophical school that sought to explain the connection between the visible world and the world of ideas and values. One of Edith's teachers, Max Scheler, was the subject of the doctoral thesis of Karol Wojtyla (Pope John Paul II). Edith transferred to the University of Göttingen during the summer semester of 1913, largely because of Husserl and her interests in his phenomenological approach. She was twenty-one years old.

Chapter 6

Phenomenology and University Life

Phenomenology, a twentieth-century philosophical movement, is an outgrowth of and response to what might be termed "modern philosophy." Through modern philosophy, with its origins in Descartes, Western civilization has come to think of human consciousness as egocentric. In this way of thinking, we cannot know the world outside our minds. We can know only our perceptions of that world. In its most extreme, "We do not know how to show that our contact with the 'real world' is not an illusion, not a mere subjective projection."[13] Such a world view is charged with consequences. Public space is diminished by the vast chasm between our own private worlds. Truth is either unknowable or relative. And philosophy cannot be ordered, as it had been in ancient and medieval philosophy, toward discovering truth. In modern philosophy, the mind is conceived as "generating truth through its own efforts.... The mind is not receptive, but creative.... [It] invents itself and constructs its truths" (Sokolowski, *Introduction to Phenomenology*, 201).

[13] Robert Sokolowski, *Introduction to Phenomenology* (Cambridge: Cambridge University Press, 2000), 10.

Edith Stein: St. Teresa Benedicta of the Cross

Phenomenology is an attempt to liberate the mind and philosophical thought from the confines of modern and now postmodern thought. Along with Thomism, phenomenology insists that a reality exists outside our minds and that we can access this reality. A phenomenologist understands that a tree can fall in the forest even if there is no one there to see or hear it fall. Since the human mind and reason are directed toward the truth of this reality, philosophy in general and phenomenology in particular provide tools for analyzing and understanding this reality. As Robert Sokolowski states, "The core doctrine of phenomenology is the teaching that every act of consciousness we perform, every experience that we have, is intentional: it is essentially 'consciousness of' or an 'experience of' something or other. All our awareness is directed toward objects" (ibid., 8). Phenomenology is the study of both our subjective intentions and the objective reality toward which these intentions are directed. It also understands that reason and truth are both present in prephilosophical thought (see ibid., 62–63).

Phenomenology, therefore, "seeks to analyze and describe the world as we experience it in persons, events, objects and concepts. The way we come to know things outside of ourselves and to gain this knowledge is through consciousness" (Irey, "Sister Benedicta," 10). In the phenomenological reduction, the philosopher steps from the "natural attitude" of intentionalities and objects into the phenomenological attitude, where he or she contemplates the various ways in which our intentions interact with the world of objects. Within

> the phenomenological attitude, we become something like detached observers of the passing scene or like spectators at a game. We become onlookers. We contemplate

the involvements we have with the world and with things in it.... But the intentionalities that we contemplate — the convictions, doubts, suspicions, certainties, and perceptions that we examine and describe — are still our intentions. We have not lost them; we only contemplate them. They remain exactly as they were and their objects remain exactly as they were, with the same correlations between intentions and objects still in force. In a very curious way, we suspend them all just as they are, we "freeze" them into place. (Sokolowski, *Introduction to Phenomenology*, 48)

This world of highly complex thought became Edith's home for the next several years as she studied under and worked for Professor Edmund Husserl. One of Edith's own contributions to this field of knowledge was her doctoral dissertation, "On the Problem of Empathy," employing the analytical tools and methods developed within the phenomenological framework.

The phenomenologist school of thought also provided fertile soil within which the seeds of ultimate truth might germinate within Edith. As Sokolowski notes, "Several followers of Husserl converted to Catholicism or Protestantism; this occurred not because Husserl encouraged such a move ..., but because his work restored respectability to various domains of experience and thus allowed people to cultivate their own religious development without hindrance" (ibid., 215). It is true that Edith did not come to faith in God's Incarnate Word through philosophy, but it is also true that far from stifling the quest for religious truth, her philosophical studies and the friendships formed during this period nurtured an openness toward the Truth, which was waiting to be discovered.

Edith Stein: St. Teresa Benedicta of the Cross

Ultimately, Edith found in phenomenology a most valid philosophical system that was to sustain her in her search for Truth, unfolding before her new horizons of knowledge—horizons to which she always remained open.

When Edith announced to her family in 1913 her plans to leave Breslau, Frau Stein voiced no objections, even if she could not understand Edith's desire to leave. "It was as though lightning had struck out of the blue. My mother said, 'If you need to go there to study, "I certainly won't bar your way.' But she was very sad—much sadder than a short absence for a summer's semester warranted. Once, in my presence, she said to little [niece] Erika: 'She doesn't like it here with us anymore'" (*Life*, 218). So Edith left for the University of Göttingen and what would be an unforeseen and challenging ascent in her life journey.

There is no doubt that Edmund Husserl was a major influence on Edith. Born to a Jewish family in 1859 in Prossnitz, Moravia, Edmund Husserl studied in Leipzig, Berlin, and Vienna. He was baptized in a Lutheran church on his twenty-seventh birthday. He came to philosophy through mathematics, qualifying as a university lecturer in Halle before becoming a professor in Göttingen. In 1900 and 1901, he published the two volumes of his *Logical Investigations* and in 1913 his *Ideas*—both works that made Husserl and his methods world-famous. The Master, as Edith and his other devoted students called him, and his writings introduced Edith to a new and unexpected world.

"Dear Göttingen!" Edith wrote, "I do believe only someone who studied there between 1905 and 1914, the short flowering time of the Göttingen School of Phenomenology, can appreciate all that the name evokes in us.... I was twenty-one years old and looked forward full of expectation to all that lay ahead" (ibid., 239).

Göttingen was, indeed, the site of the beginning of a new phase in Edith's life—or as Husserl calls these, "new horizons." Here she encountered the world of faith and first came into contact with the Catholic Faith in a thinker of rank, Max Scheler. This community of thinkers brought Edith into a religious atmosphere of intellectuals who had a deep spirituality. Edith eventually reasoned that the world of faith had to be worthy of consideration, since people she admired and considered superior to her lived lives of faith.

Although many of her teachers and fellow academics had been born Jewish and became Christian, Edith's niece Susanne Batzdorff dismisses the idea that Edith would embrace another religion merely because of another person's influence. "We have seen that Edith was not one to follow the advice or suggestions of friends or relatives, if she did not share their views," Batzdorff wrote in *Aunt Edith*. "She would surely not do so now, unless her studies and search took her in a direction that led to another faith. . . . Edith, a seeker after truth from way back, encountered in this new environment a liberating spirit that gave her permission, as it were, to embark on a new and independent path and look for new truths, unencumbered by the conditioning of home and family, which were now far away" (*Aunt Edith*, 116).

The phenomenological method that Husserl presented to Edith had "a positive influence on her research into the essence of things, freeing her from narrow preconceptions and leading her to a state of total impartiality." Without phenomenology, "she would have been incapable of opening herself to the thought of God with that absolute objectivity of judgment so characteristic of her."[14]

---

[14] "St. Teresa Benedicta of the Cross—Edith Stein" (1998), posted on the website of the Discalced Carmelites, http://www.ocd.pcn. net/ed_en.htm.

Although he did not lead her to the Faith, Max Scheler and his "Catholic ideas" opened for her "a region of 'phenomena' which I could then no longer bypass blindly," Edith wrote. "This was my first encounter with this hitherto totally unknown world.... With good reason we were repeatedly enjoined [in the Husserl school] to observe all things without prejudice, to discard all possible 'blinders.' The barriers of rationalistic prejudices with which I had unwittingly grown up fell, and the world of faith unfolded before me.... Persons with whom I associated daily, whom I esteemed and admired, lived in it. At the least, they deserved my giving it some serious reflection" (*Life*, 260).

This new knowledge and understanding, however, resulted in pressing questions for Edith. "She wanted to clarify the religious problem, to understand what relationship there could be (or there *should* be) between herself and God," the Carmelite essay noted. "To interpret this relationship as an abstraction seemed to her absurd, inclined as she was to relate everything to concrete reality. Should she then imagine the relationship idealistically or romantically? That could never be for her, always striving to grasp things in their deepest essence, without which nothing had value in her eyes. Would it be easier then to discount the existence of God? But Edith was never one to choose the easy way. In her whole life she always chose the tough ascent." But as Edith herself pointed out, she did not "embark on a systematic investigation of the questions of faith; I was far too busy with other matters. I was content to accept without resistance the stimuli coming from my surroundings, and so, almost without noticing it, became gradually transformed" (ibid., 260–261).

Edith's sister Erna and a friend, who later became Erna's husband, visited Edith in Göttingen following their medical state board examinations. "We spent an unforgettable time, with delightful excursions and hours of fun in which [Edith] did her best to show us her beloved Göttingen and its attractive environs at their best. Following that visit, we took a hike through the very beautiful Harz Mountains. That was in Spring, 1914" (ibid., 16).

Edith loved nature and the outdoors and often took long hikes and picnics with her friends. On Saturday afternoons, "weather permitting," recalled Edith,

> we went out into the country.... On Sundays when the weather was good, we were usually outdoors all day. Sometimes we were out from Saturday noon until Sunday evening. After all, we intended to ... get to know the countryside of central Germany. Göttingen was an excellent starting point for doing so. To the southeast, the town hugs a hill; the Bismarck Tower is on its crest. Beautiful parks stretch upward from the town limits. They extend all the way to the Göttingen Forest through which one can walk for a whole day without reaching its end, and usually, too, without meeting anyone at all.... For lengthier excursions, we took our provisions in rucksacks; and in the woods we made our meal of a loaf of pumpernickel, a jar of butter, some cold cuts, fruit, and chocolate. All this pleased us more than a dinner at the inn. Hills and woods surround Göttingen on the other sides as well. The ample beech forests were aglow in red and gold when one arrived in the autumn for the winter semester. Old ruined castles, perched on the heights, peer into the valley. I was particularly fond of the 'Gleichen,' two hill-tops directly side by side, both crowned with ruins.... When we looked down into the valley from

that height, I had such a feeling of being in the heart of Germany: a lovely landscape on the slopes, carefully husbanded fields, neat villages, and an encircling wreath of green forests. (ibid., 243–244)

During her college years at Göttingen, Edith developed deep friendships, several of them with male friends—and almost all of them the source of speculation regarding marriage by various biographers. All of these friends mentioned, Edith tells us—"although they studied additional subjects"—were members of the Philosophical Society at Göttingen. For them, "philosophy was the virtual life-element" (ibid., 255). Susanne Batzdorff believes that her aunt appeared serious about one young man in particular, Hans Lipps. "Hans Lipps made a deeper impression on me than did anyone else," Edith recalled later.

Twenty-three years old at the time, he looked much younger. Very tall, slim, but powerfully built, he had a handsome, expressive face, lively as a child's. His gaze was serious; still his large, round eyes were as inquisitive as a child's.... We were all convinced that his insights were true and deep even though we were incapable of confirming them ourselves. When he had difficulty in expressing himself in words, his eyes and his lively, spontaneous facial expressions spoke all the more persuasively.... He was unable to keep up regular attendance on these evenings [of the Philosophical Society] since he was preparing simultaneously for his preliminary exams in medicine and, with a thesis on plant physiology, for his doctorate in philosophy. Studying medicine and natural science was his way of filling in the hours during which one could not philosophize. (ibid., 254)

While at first Edith describes him "only in terms of their relationship as fellow students," Batzdorff recounted, "a friendship developed, and in 1915, during his military service in the First World War, Edith sent him packages.... No letters have been preserved from Hans Lipps to Edith Stein and her reticence in personal matters prevented her from discussing her feelings about him, but from a letter by her friend Hedwig Conrad-Martius we know that Edith kept a photograph of Lipps on her desk.... Although Hans Lipps married in 1923, he and Edith remained friends, and, after the death of his wife in 1932, he proposed marriage to her. By then, Edith said, it was too late. She had found another path" (*Aunt Edith*, 184–185).

That Edith did not marry or proclaim herself serious about any young man was, ultimately, the consequence of her own decision. "Although she does not refer to this in her [family's biography]," explained its translator, Sister Josephine Koeppel, "there are very clear indications in her letters that it was her free choice" (*Life*, 455). From her conversion on, "consideration of marriage with anyone was out of the question for her. It was 'too late' simply because she was so certain that she had received a call to become a contemplative nun.... For Edith, the call to Carmel was already a commitment; every word we read after January 1, 1922, when Edith was baptized in the Catholic church in Bergzabern, bears out her fidelity to that call" (ibid., 457).

Edith studied with Husserl from the summer semester of 1913 until July 30, 1914, when lectures at Göttingen were canceled at the outbreak of the war.

Chapter 7

The War to End All Wars

In the meantime, the Great War—the war that would become known as the First World War—broke out, and Edith's spirit joined the great patriotism that stirred the Jews of Germany. She immediately left her philosophical studies to train as a Red Cross assistant nurse, although she was not immediately needed. When her friend, teacher, and fellow philosopher Adolf Reinach was asked if he, too, must go to war, Reinach reportedly replied, "It's not that I must; rather, I'm permitted to go." His statement "pleased me very much," Edith noted. "It expressed so well my own feelings" (*Life*, 294).

"No one growing up during or since the war can possibly imagine the security in which we assumed ourselves to be living before 1914," Edith wrote of that turbulent period in history. "Our life was built on an indestructible foundation of peace, stability of ownership of property, and on the permanence of circumstances to which we were accustomed.... Now I rushed back to my rooms, packed what was essential for the immediate future, stowed everything else away in a hamper which my landlady was to keep in storage.... I would go to the Red Cross" (ibid., 293, 296). From her home in Breslau, a few days later, she added, "'I have no private life anymore,' I told myself. 'All my energy must be devoted to this great happening. Only when the war is over, if I'm alive then, will I be permitted to think of my private affairs once more.' The next day was the Sunday on which [we learned that] war was declared" (ibid., 297).

Auguste Stein showed "great opposition" and tried to forbid her daughter Edith from volunteering with the Red Cross, finally telling her, "You will not go with my permission." But Edith remained equally determined, replying, "Then I must go without your permission." Edith's sisters were "shocked at my harsh retort," Edith remembered in writing. "My mother was totally unaccustomed to such opposition.... Now, however, granite was striking granite. My mother said no more and was very silent and depressed for several days ... but when subsequently I began making my preparations, she, as a matter of course, undertook to provide the complete nurse's outfit called for" (ibid., 319).

Since she was not immediately called for service by the Red Cross, Edith returned to Göttingen for another semester with Husserl, taking—and passing—in January 1915 her *Staatsexamen pro faculte docendi*. That spring Edith was finally called up by the Red Cross and assigned for work at the cadet academy—which had been converted into a lazaretto, or hospital for infectious diseases—at Mährisch-Weisskirchen (now Hranice), the Moravian sector of the Carpathian war front. There Edith served for several months as an assistant nurse to soldiers of the Austrian army infected with spotted fever, dysentery, cholera, and typhoid. The hospital was administered and staffed by the German Red Cross as the German army that winter sought to drive back the Russians, who were advancing on Hungary.

"I got the impression that the sick were not used to getting loving attention," Edith reflected, "and that volunteer helpers therefore could find endless opportunities to show their own compassion and love of neighbor in these places of suffering" (ibid., 298). Edith "felt obliged to interrupt her studies to go to a field hospital in Mährisch-Weisskirchen as a volunteer Red Cross aide," remembered her sister Erna. "There, as everywhere else, she was engrossed wholeheartedly in her work and was equally popular with the wounded soldiers, her colleagues, and her superiors. There too, I visited her during my first wartime leave and spent two weeks with her" (ibid., 16).

It was clearly Edith's desire "to disappear into devotion to a greater good," as writer Patricia Hampl notes in her Edith Stein essay. "What appealed to her was the surrender of individual life to a massive reality encompassing everyone.... Ultimately, a life seeking greatness is about the loss of the self in the service of a more complete reality. It is a disappearing act. It is, sometimes, a martyrdom. That, finally, is how it came to be in the unlikely life of Edith Stein" (*Stories*, 104–105).

Although previously rejected as unfit to serve in the military, Adolf Hitler also volunteered at the onset of World War I. He joined the 16th Bavarian Reserve Infantry Regiment and was wounded in October 1916, and gassed two years later. Hitler was still hospitalized when the war ended in 1918. Except when hospitalized, he was continuously in the front line as a headquarters runner. Hitler's bravery in action was rewarded with the Iron Cross, Second Class, in December 1914, and the Iron Cross, First Class (a rare decoration for a corporal), in August 1918.

For her nursing stint at Mährisch-Weisskirchen and "in recognition of her selfless service," Edith received the medal of valor.[15]

---

[15] Waltraud Herbstrith, O.C.D., *Edith Stein: A Biography* (San Francisco: Ignatius Press, 1985), 53.

Chapter 8

＠

Back to the World of Academia

In January 1915, at Göttingen, Edith had passed the state boards for teaching preparatory philosophy, history, and German. Following her work at the hospital for infectious diseases, Edith returned to Breslau, where she prepared her thesis and substituted from February until October 1916 for a secondary-school teacher who was ill. Although she reported again to the Red Cross as available for assignment, she was never again called up for service. The Mährisch-Weisskirchen lazaretto, no longer in the military zone, had by then been closed.

During those months in Breslau, Edith led an arduous schedule that combined teaching with demanding doctoral research. "Upon coming home from school, I put all my school matters aside and took up my doctoral work," she wrote years later in her family's biography. "The family got to see me at the evening meal; but as soon as it was over, I withdrew again. Only at about ten at night would I begin preparing the following day's classes. If, while doing so, I became so fatigued that I could no longer grasp anything, I would read a bit of Shakespeare. That so renewed my vitality that I was able to begin again. Before going to bed, my mother would come in to me ... and she would leave after a good-night kiss. But she always saw to it that I had some refreshment for this nocturnal labor. If the family had some fruit, then a small plateful of bite-size pieces was prepared and set before me on the desk. Besides that, Rosa had a supply of cookies and chocolate in some hidden place; and she brought me some of it every night. Gradually, despite all this, the results of the continued pressure became noticeable.... This led me to the realization that in the long run a combination of teaching with simultaneous, serious research was impossible" (*Life*, 396).

In spite of her professional income, as always, Edith's major source of income, which allowed her to continue her studies, was an allowance from her mother.

In the meantime, Professor Husserl, the Master, was appointed to the University of Freiburg-im-Breisgau in April of 1916—which meant that Edith, too, had to follow him there in order to take her doctoral examination. It was the first time that Edith would cross to the south of the River Main. "I had no knowledge at all of southern Germany as yet," she wrote in her memoirs, "and had long wished to go there. The sojourn in Freiburg was to be my vacation as well."

On the way to Freiburg to take the orals for her doctorate, Edith arranged to meet and travel part of the way with her old friend Hans Lipps. "We exchanged news about the others in our circle," Edith remembered later. "In the course of this exchange, he asked me: 'Do you also belong to this "club" in Munich that goes to Mass every day?' I could not help but laugh at his amusing way of expressing it, although at the same time, I keenly minded his lack of respect." Lipps was referring to colleagues whom they both knew from philosophical circles who had become Catholic converts and were now, in Edith's words, "very zealous. 'No, I was not one of them,'" she told Lipps. "Very nearly I added,

'Unfortunately.' 'Actually, Fraulein Stein, what's it all about? I don't understand any of it.' I understood a little but was unable to say much about it" (ibid., 398–399).

On August 3, 1916, twenty-four-year-old Edith not only passed her oral exams to earn a doctorate in philosophy but did so summa cum laude—with highest honors. "That evening we were invited to the Husserls'.... Frau Husserl and Elli [her daughter] had wound ivy and daisies into a gorgeous wreath. This was set on my head in place of a laurel wreath.... Husserl was beaming with joy" (ibid., 413–414). Edith also arranged to work with Husserl as his academic assistant beginning that October. "His delight at the thought of now having a person entirely at his disposal was apparent," Edith wrote in a letter to a friend a couple of weeks later, "although, obviously, he has no clear idea as yet how we will actually work together. In any case we are agreed that first of all we are going to get at the manuscripts of *Ideen*. In preparation for this, I have to learn Gabelsberger shorthand, since that is the key to the holy of holies."[16]

That August found Edith studying Gabelsberger shorthand, the system Edmund Husserl used to write his notes, in preparation for their work together. Edith also inaugurated what she referred to as a "Philosophical Kindergarten," an introductory class meant to acquaint novices with the Master's phenomenology and his methods. While many of her friends still suffered at the war front, Edith finished her teaching duties in Breslau and began working with Husserl. She brought some order to Husserl's many research manuscripts, taking part in transcribing his essays

---

[16] Edith Stein, *Self-Portrait in Letters: 1916–1942*, ed. L. Gelber and Romaeus Leuven, O.C.D., trans. Josephine Koeppel, O.C.D. (Washington, DC: ICS Publications, 1993), 2.

and works in progress from Gabelsberger shorthand and arranging the piles of folio in a systematic order. Her dissertation, "On the Problem of Empathy," and her successful oral examination in 1916 earned her the degree of doctor of philosophy, conferred on her on March 30, 1917. That same spring, several chapters of her dissertation were published in German in Halle, Germany.

That summer, Erna once again touched base with her childhood "twin." "Two of our old friends, Rose Guttmann and Lilli Platau, and I decided to spend our 1917 summer vacation with her in the Black Forest. (In the meantime I had gone to Berlin as a medical resident.) Those days are one of the times which remain a shining memory, although we all felt depressed by the war, and the somewhat frugal diet could have affected our mood," Erna wrote years later. "We hiked, read together and, for the most part, had a lot of fun. The following year I returned to Breslau and had to take my vacation alone this time. Again I could think of no better plan than to visit Edith. We stayed in Freiburg, took several wonderful trips from there, read together and made plans for our future" (ibid., 17).

Adolf Reinach, Edith's beloved friend and teacher, died in November of 1917, at the war front. It was Reinach's death, ironically, that formulated a decisive moment in Edith's road to conversion. Edith went to see his widow, Anna Reinach, fearful that she would find a broken and distraught woman. Instead, Edith found a committed Christian, suffering, but at peace. Edith said later, "It was my first encounter with the Cross and the divine power that it bestows on those who carry it. For the first time, I was seeing with my very eyes the Church, born from her Redeemer's sufferings, triumphant over the sting of death. That was the moment my unbelief collapsed and Christ shone forth—in the mystery of the Cross" (Herbstrith, *Edith Stein*, 56). As Father

Johannes Hirschmann reportedly noted in a letter of May 3, 1950, to the Mother Superior at the Cologne Carmel, "Sister Teresa Benedicta herself distinguished between the cause of her conversion to Christianity and the cause of her entrance to the Catholic Church.... The most decisive reason for her conversion to Christianity was, as she told me, the way and manner in which her friend Mrs. Reinach made her offer in the power of the mystery of the cross after her husband died at the front during the First World War."[17]

During this time, Edith, still searching for what she could not yet name, was taken aback by an experience that forever remained with her. On one of her trips, Edith met her friend Pauline Reinach in Frankfurt, and the two women strolled through the old section of the city as they visited. While visiting the cathedral, Edith saw a woman who had obviously been shopping come into the empty church and kneel silently in a pew. Edith had never seen this before, having seen people praying only during services in Protestant churches and Jewish synagogues. "We stopped in at the cathedral for a few minutes; and, while we looked around in respectful silence, a woman carrying a market basket came in and knelt down in one of the pews to pray briefly. This was something entirely new to me.... Here was someone interrupting her everyday shopping errands to come into this church, although no other person was in it, as though she were here for an intimate conversation. I could never forget that" (*Life*, 401).

A seed of faith, in the meantime, had been planted within Edith, but it would take time to germinate. As the editor notes

---

[17] Freda Mary Oben, Ph.D., *Edith Stein: Scholar, Feminist, Saint* (Staten Island, NY: Alba House, 1988), 15.

in a follow-up chronology added to *Life in a Jewish Family*, "At fifteen, Edith decided she did not believe in God; at twenty-four, when she gave herself to phenomenology, the first flicker of faith began to dart into view. Most of her peers at Göttingen were Christian. So, too, were Husserl and Max Scheler. In 1918, faith's spark was so strong that Edith had to live by it, despite her realization that it might cost her the love and understanding of her family and friends. Faithful to her commitment in her search for the fullness of truth, by 1920, Edith was discerning whether to follow Christ in the Catholic or the Evangelical (Lutheran) Church" (ibid., 420).

Although her year and a half with Husserl was a difficult time for Edith, who wanted more joint technical projects than Husserl seemed interested in, he remained for her "the Master, whose image cannot be blurred by any human weakness" (*Self-Portrait*, 37–38). In letters to her friend Roman Ingarden, Edith confides over and over her dissatisfaction with her work, as the Master found no time to review the work that Edith painstakingly put in order. Finally, early in 1918, Edith asked Husserl to dispense her from her role as his personal assistant. She wrote to Ingarden, "The Master has graciously accepted my resignation. His letter was most friendly—though not without a somewhat reproachful undertone. So now I am free, and I believe it is good that I am, even if, for the moment, I am not exactly happy . . ." (ibid., 23). And to her friend Fritz Kaufmann, Edith explained, "Putting manuscripts in order, which was all my work consisted of for months, was gradually getting to be unbearable for me, nor does it seem to me to be so necessary that, for its sake, I should have to renounce doing anything on my own" (ibid.).

Edith's journey toward faith continued, her heart opening more and more to the goodness of God's love. As Germany

suffered political and military defeat in "the war to end all wars,"
tragedy struck close to home. In a letter dated July 6, 1918, and
addressed to her sister Erna in Breslau, Edith hoped to affirm and
encourage Erna and Rosa after the death of one of their friends:

> I would like so much to instill in both of you some of what,
> after every new blow, gives me fresh strength. I can only
> say that after everything I went through in the past year,
> I affirm life more than ever.... I really believe, at times,
> that one has to get accustomed to the idea of possibly not
> living to see the end of this war. Even then, one may not
> despair. One should not restrict one's view merely to the
> particle of life that is within one's ken, much less to what
> lies clearly apparent on the surface. After all, it is quite
> certain that we are at a turning point in the evolution
> of the intellectual life of humankind; and one may not
> complain if the crisis lasts longer than is acceptable to the
> individual. Everything that is now so terrible, and that I
> have no intention of glossing over, is precisely the spirit
> that must be surmounted. But the new spirit already exists
> and will prevail beyond all doubt. It may be clearly seen
> in philosophy and in the beginning of the new art form
> of expressionism. As surely as materialism and naturalism
> have become outmoded here, just as surely will they be-
> come obsolete in all the other spheres of life, even though
> slowly and amid painful struggles. One senses the will
> for this also in the political and social struggles that are
> driven by motives that differ totally from the hackneyed
> slogans people are wont to ascribe to them. Good and
> evil, knowledge and ignorance are mixed on *all* sides, and
> each one sees only the positive of his own side and the

negative of the others'. That holds for peoples as well as
parties. All this, intertwined, is spinning madly so no one
can tell when some calm and clarity will set in again. In
any case, life is much too complex for anyone to impose
on it even the most clever plan for bettering the world,
nor can one prescribe finally and unequivocally how it
should proceed. (*Self-Portrait*, 27)

Early in 1919, a young Adolf Hitler returned from a military
hospital to Munich, where he underwent a course of systematic
political education that featured nationalism, anti-Semitism,
and anti-socialism. Later that year, in what is considered his
first explicit anti-Semitic writing—and the first written document of his political career—Hitler wrote in a letter, "And thus
arises this fact, that amongst us lives a non-German, foreign
race, which is neither willing nor capable of sacrificing its racial
characteristics, nor to renounce its own way of feeling, thinking
and striving. Nevertheless, it possesses all the political rights we
do.... The Jew's cause in effect turns into a racial tuberculosis of
the nations." Hitler proclaimed, "The final goal [of rational anti-
Semitism] has to be the irrevocable removal of Jews in general."[18]

Edith had hopes for *Habilitation*, a professional position on
a university philosophy faculty, which seemed to be in vain.
The academic profession was not open to women—and Husserl
himself refused a proper recommendation on grounds of gender.
Nevertheless, Edith continued to work independently on the second thesis required to win appointment as a university teacher.
She also taught in Breslau, giving private instruction to college

[18] Adolf Hitler, *Hitler: Sämtliche Aufzeichnungen 1905–1924*, ed. Eberhard Jäckel, trans. Peter Keupen (Stuttgart: Deutsche Verlags-
Anstalt, 1980), 89–90.

and university students, writing articles and essays, and lecturing, a career that continued to escalate during the next decade. "Edith Stein's aims for a university career were thwarted because, in her lifetime, the prejudices against women and Jews stood like an immovable wall between her and academic advancement," summarized her niece Susanne Batzdorff. "Her doctorate, passed with highest honors, her early successes in her field, her acclaim as a lecturer, her diligence as a translator and author, were all nipped in the bud, and her future in all these areas cut off" (*Aunt Edith*, 68–69). In 1919, the Göttingen faculty declined even to consider the required work on a second thesis of a woman. Instead, back in Breslau, Edith devoted herself to private lessons in phenomenology and to her writing.

In March 1921, Edith left Breslau for Göttingen and on to Bergzabern, where she would stay most of the year with her friends Theodor and Hedwig Conrad-Martius, both philosophers and students of Husserl — and a regular meeting place for former pupils of Husserl.

Chapter 9

⁀

Struggling into Faith: Conversion

Perhaps it was the fact that Teresa of Avila's great-grandfather was a Spanish Jew who converted to Christianity, although Edith would not have known this historical fact. Perhaps it was seeing her own reflection in a soul's earnest search for God. Perhaps it was something else that we are unable to guess. Whatever the reason, something drew Edith to that particular book, on that particular shelf, on an evening alone at the Conrads' home in Bergzabern in the Palatinate while on vacation with her university colleagues during the summer of 1921.

About to turn thirty years old, Edith immersed herself in the autobiography of the sixteenth-century mystic and Carmelite reformer Teresa of Avila, and she experienced a swift conversion. Fascinated, Edith read the book in one night, proclaiming simply, "This is the truth!" Her "long search for the true faith" simply and suddenly came to an end. As Carmelite Sister Maria Amata Neyer remarks in her photo book on Edith's life, for years Edith had looked for truth philosophically, as a scholar. "It was the 'truth of things,' the 'things themselves,' the objects. Now in Teresa of Avila she was filled with the truth of love that is not knowledge, but relationship. Teresa lived in mystical friendship with God and with him whom God had sent, Jesus Christ."[19] The next day, Edith bought a missal and a copy of the Catholic catechism.

As her niece Susanne Batzdorff notes, whenever someone asked Edith, the woman once described by her family as "a book with seven seals," why she became a Catholic or why she chose Carmel as her destination, "she would reply in Latin, *Secretum meum mihi* (This secret belongs to me)" (*Aunt Edith*, 116–117). Edith alluded to her "changes" in a letter to her friend Fritz Kaufmann: "I found the place where there is rest and peace for all restless hearts. How that happened is something you will allow me to be silent about today. I am not reluctant to speak about it and, at the right time, will surely do so with you also, but it has to 'come about'; it is not something about which I can 'report' in a letter" (*Self-Portrait*, 47).

In fact, there is no personal essay, no biographical note, not even a mention in a letter—nothing—that elaborates or explains what led Edith to take such swift and determined action. What we do know is that the same woman who at the age of seven suddenly underwent what she called a "great transformation," now experienced an immediate and decisive adult conversion. "What had happened to her, what continued to happen to her, thanks to the daily grace of liturgical and contemplative prayer, was a mystery. It was simply to be lived," writes Patricia Hampl in her Edith Stein essay. "What she found in Teresa she also kept to herself, though certainly she is not the first person to have been profoundly affected by that ardent personality. Even today, almost four and a half centuries since she wrote it, Teresa's

[19] Maria Amata Neyer, O.C.D., *Edith Stein: Her Life in Photos and Documents* (Washington, DC: ICS Publications, 1999), 34.

autobiography remains one of the most vivid personal documents in the history of Christian testimony, at least as spirited as Saint Augustine's *Confessions*, and more charming. These three — Augustine, Teresa, Edith — form a fascinating linked chain of conversions, each in turn liberated from what Teresa calls in her autobiography, 'the shadow of death,' which left them utterly worn out with interior struggle" (*Stories*, 114–115).

Carmelite Sister Waltraud Herbstrith, one of Edith Stein's early biographers, points out that Edith's experience with Teresa — honored as a Doctor of the Catholic Church — was, in fact, no different from what had happened to Teresa herself four centuries earlier when reading St. Augustine. The "shadow of death" experienced by each of them was different; yet their conversion came as they learned to surrender what was keeping them from God. "It makes no difference what particular form this 'shadow' assumes — sensuality as with Augustine, or worldly contacts as with Teresa, or attachment to a rationalist world view, as with Edith Stein," writes Herbstrith. "All that is necessary for conversion to take place is that the individual honestly comes to recognize that his 'death' is depriving him of the freedom to offer himself to God. Honesty and freedom, to Edith Stein, had always constituted the two greatest challenges imposed on the human person. Now she found them appearing with equal prominence in Saint Teresa" (Herbstrith, *Edith Stein*, 66).

While everything looked the same from the outside, Edith was forever changed on the inside. She became a woman of prayer, aware that, as St. Teresa points out, interior prayer is the setting where that healing and transformation take place. During the fall of 1921, she returned to the family home in Breslau. Edith stayed to assist Erna, who was expecting her first child, with running the household.

Edith Stein: St. Teresa Benedicta of the Cross

While in Breslau, Edith attended Mass every morning. "In September 1921 our first child, Susanne, was born, and Edith, who happened to be at home just then, looked after me most devotedly," recalled Erna. "However, a deep shadow overcast that otherwise happy time; Edith confided to me her decision to become a Catholic and asked me to get Mother used to the idea. I knew this was one of the most difficult tasks I had ever faced. As much as my mother had shown understanding for everything and left us children a wide range of freedom in all matters, this decision of Edith was the most severe blow for Mother, for she was a truly devout Jewess. She considered Edith's adoption of another religion an act of deep disloyalty. The rest of us were hit hard, also, but we had such great confidence in Edith's innermost conviction that we accepted her decision with a heavy heart after trying in vain to talk her out of it for our mother's sake" (*Life*, 17).

On New Year's Day, 1922, thirty-year-old Edith Stein wore a black dress and had a white mantle around her as baptismal water was poured on her head (see *Self-Portrait*, 105). In addition to baptism, she received her first Communion that day from Father Eugen Breitling at the parish church of St. Martin, taking on the Christian names of Theresia and Hedwig. Her sponsor was her friend, Hedwig Conrad-Martius. Edith often said that from the day of her baptism, it had always been her intention to enter the order of her beloved St. Teresa—when the time was right.

Edith's mother suffered deeply over the conversion of her daughter, which was one of the central reasons for Edith's decision to wait to enter the monastery. "She particularly rejects conversions," Edith noted of her mother's attitude in a 1933 letter to a friend, which also discussed Edith's entrance into Carmel. "Everyone ought to live and die in the faith in which they were born. She imagines atrocious things about Catholicism and life in a convent. At the moment it is difficult to know what is causing her more pain: whether it is the separation from her youngest child to whom she has ever been attached with a particular love, or her horror of the completely foreign and inaccessible world into which that child is disappearing, or the qualms of conscience that she herself is at fault because she was not strict enough in raising me as a Jew" (ibid., 160). But Edith's eleven-year wait between baptism and entrance into Carmel was also out of obedience to her spiritual directors, who no doubt also realized that Edith's talents as lecturer and teacher were much needed in their volatile world.

On February 2, 1922, Edith was confirmed in the private chapel of the bishop of Speyer, Bishop Ludwig Sebastian. Through her wise spiritual adviser and friend, Monsignor Josef Schwind, vicar-general of the Diocese of Speyer, Edith became acquainted with the Dominican convent of St. Magdalena's. It was Monsignor Schwind's direction that led Edith to postpone the thought of entering religious life "until it would become unmistakably evident that this was God's will for her" (*Life*, 421).

Instead, she accepted a position in Speyer teaching at the schools run by the Dominican Sisters and took private vows (see Oben, *Edith Stein*, 21). At St. Magdalena's, Edith was able to live in a room adjacent to the nuns' quarters rather than among the students, enabling her to attend daily Mass, pray the Divine Office with the Sisters, and to participate in quiet hours of meditation. This became her work and home for the next eight years. As Patricia Hampl says in her essay on Stein, "In effect, she managed to mimic a monastic life years before her entrance into Carmel" (*Stories*, 114). In a letter a few years into her stay in Speyer, Edith states, "For all of three years now I have been living behind the sheltering walls of a convent, at heart—and this I may surely say without any presumption—like a real nun, even though I wear no veil and am not bound by vows or enclosure. Nor for the present, may I think of contracting such a bond" (*Self-Portrait*, 47).

After Edith became a Catholic she continued to visit home regularly. To her family, including a large number of nieces and nephews, Tante Edith still occupied a special place in the family. "She was, for the most part, an absentee aunt, even before she became a Carmelite," noted Batzdorff. "But she wrote regularly to all her nieces and nephews. And my brother and I enjoyed reading the humorous playlet she composed for our parents' wedding, and participating with our cousins in the dance skit she prepared for Grandmother Stein's 80th birthday. When she came to visit, her presence immediately made itself felt. As my brother once put it, she brought a holiday atmosphere with her. To us, she was not a figure of other-worldly scholarly solemnity, but a friend with a delightful sense of humor who could be relied on for annual visits" (*Selected Writings*, 108).

Erna recalled, "[Edith] took care of me again after the birth of our son Ernst Ludwig [1922], and she tenderly loved both children, just as she loved all our nephews and nieces, and was loved and revered by them in return. I remember especially how often, when she was working in her study, she had one of the children with her, how she would give them a book to look at, and how happy and contented they were" (*Life*, 17–18).

Edith often wrote plays, poems, and skits, enlisting the assistance of her nephews and nieces as performers, to celebrate special occasions, such as the skit she created for her sister Erna's wedding. She also enjoyed giving of herself by providing her family and friends with personal items with a special meaning to her that she hoped they, too, would enjoy. "From her collection of books, which remained in Grandmother's house, I received a volume on each birthday as a gift from my aunt," Batzdorff remembered. "I still cherish these mementos, which include Rainer Maria Rilke's 'Stories of God' and a collection of Hans Christian Andersen. Another treasured keepsake is a message she [inscribed in my autograph book] on Aug. 20, 1933, just before she became a nun. It is a quotation from the 27th Psalm. In a time of fear and uncertainty, a time for me of confusion and doubt, she had written: 'The Lord is my light and my salvation; whom shall I fear?'" (*Selected Writings*, 110).

Chapter 10

⌒

On Being Woman

Most of Edith Stein's writing on women and women's vocation stems from her lectures, which took place during the decade of her professional life between her conversion and her entrance into the Carmelite community. Much of it (1923–1931) was spent at Speyer, where Edith promoted the comprehensive formation of women, sharing with them not only a knowledge of Christ but also of the tasks that would confront them later in life in professional work and marriage. Edith challenged her students with the knowledge that, as women, they are created in the image of God in their equality and in their diversity.

In her student years at Breslau and Göttingen, Edith called herself a feminist and an advocate for women's right to vote and for working women's education. "As that rare phenomenon, the woman philosopher, she inspires women to the highest intellectual and professional achievement," wrote the biographer and English translator of Edith Stein's *Essays on Woman*, Dr. Freda Mary Oben. "[Stein] points to the interior life, the life of prayer and contemplation as the source of strength. In line with some of the women in scripture, Stein is a Jewish heroine, as well as a holy Christian. . . . She demonstrates that the truths of the

Edith Stein: St. Teresa Benedicta of the Cross

Christian faith are more than abstractions; she experienced these and lived them passionately.... As a woman of intellectual and spiritual stature, she is a witness to authentic feminism."[20]

"God has given each human being a threefold destiny: to grow into the likeness of God through the development of his faculties, to procreate descendants, and to hold dominion over the earth," Edith wrote. "In addition, it is promised that a life of faith and personal union with the Redeemer will be rewarded by eternal contemplation of God. These destinies, natural and supernatural, are identical for both man and woman." While "natural forces" can and often do counteract the mother's duties "even when she amply indicates a genuine intention for good family life, a spirit of self-sacrifice and of inner growth," Edith emphasized in her discourse, there is an "inexhaustible source of power" available to all, "the grace of God. It depends only on knowing one's way and going to this source again and again. There is always a way open to each of the faithful: the way of prayer. Whoever sincerely believes in the words 'Ask and you shall receive,' is given consolation and courage to persevere in every need. Even if it is not the immediate help which, to some extent, the person conceives of and desires, help does come" (*Essays on Woman*, 100, 120).

Edith was very concerned about the role of women in society and the Church. As the Carmelite Priors General noted in their essay posted online, "[Edith's] intellectual capacity, university and professional training, her dedication to teaching, made her a woman who, from a conscious female identity, experienced the challenges of a mission.... She was able to demonstrate the

[20] Edith Stein, *Essays on Woman*, trans. Freda Mary Oben (Washington, DC: ICS Publications, 1996), xi.

richness of a female Christian life devoted to fulfilling a mission forming part of the real world.... In her work as teacher, she knew how to combine professional competence with a direct, personal relationship with her pupils. They always remember her as an open-minded, understanding woman, ahead of her times in recognizing the true value of women and in her generous commitment to promoting women in all aspects" (Maccise and Chalmers, "Losing to Win").

In reality, teaching was not part of Edith's vision for her own life. As she explained in a letter to an old friend, "I do not take myself too seriously as a teacher, and still have to smile when I have to put it down anywhere as my profession. But that does not hinder me from taking my responsibilities seriously, and so, in spirit and soul, I am deeply absorbed by them" (*Self-Portrait*, 47). Yet by 1932, Edith Stein was recognized as "the intellectual leader of Catholic feminism in Europe," wrote Oben. "She delivered lectures constantly, which later became *Die Frau*, for the League of Catholic Women and the Association of Catholic Women Teachers. These groups actually formed the Catholic Women's Movement. She became their 'voice,' speaking at their annual conventions, acting as their advisor in plans of reform and in discussions with government officials" (*Edith Stein*, 23).

Her lectures on women's roles incorporated the roles of women as professionals, responsible coworkers in the Church, homemakers, teachers, and mothers. "Edith went 'beyond sociology, psychology, and philosophy' in her treatment of the problems of our time, but she did so not by ignoring these disciplines but by placing them within the faith dimension in which she presented her suggested solutions," wrote the translator of *Life in a Jewish Family*. "She shared the fruits of both, her years of association with important thinkers, and her wide human experience; and she did this sharing in a heartfelt simple manner as one who had deep empathy for her hearers and their challenging situations. She awoke the conscience of teachers and parents, but did not leave them without the means for waging their own contest" (*Life*, 419).

The motivation for these inquiries into the nature and vocation of women stemmed from "the need to educate women in a way that would be perfective of them, not just as generic human beings, but as women," noted journalist Laura Garcia in her article on Edith Stein. "Stein rejected the radical feminist claim that there are no important differences between men and women. As a philosopher looking for the basis of true femininity, she begins with what might be called an ontology of woman."[21]

Along with St. Thomas and Aristotle, Edith acknowledged that there are indeed traits unique to the human soul shared by every member of the species. But "if the soul is the form of the body, and the form of humanity is individuated by being united with this body or that one, Stein reasoned that the woman's soul will have a spiritual quality distinct from the man's soul. She did not argue that biology is destiny, but that the physical differences between men and women profoundly mark their personalities," Garcia explained. "The woman's body stamps her soul with particular qualities that are *common* to all women but *different* from distinctively masculine traits. Stein saw these differences as complementary and not hierarchical in value, and so they should be recognized and celebrated rather than minimized and deplored. There are two ways of being human, as man or as woman" (Garcia, "Edith Stein," 21).

[21] Laura Garcia, "Edith Stein—Convert, Nun, Martyr," *Crisis* (June 1997): 21.

On Being Woman

In Edith's mind, ultimately, differences between males and females are a matter of common sense and in need of little argument. "Only the person blinded by the passion of controversy could deny that woman in soul and body is formed for a particular purpose," Edith wrote. "The clear and irrevocable word of Scripture declares what daily experience teaches from the beginning of the world: woman is destined to be wife and mother. Both physically and spiritually she is endowed for this purpose.... Of course, woman shares a basic human nature, but basically her faculties are different from men; therefore, a differing type of soul must exist as well.... Woman naturally seeks to embrace that which is *living, personal and whole*. To cherish, guard, protect, nourish and advance growth is her natural, maternal yearning.... *Abstraction* in *every sense* is alien to the feminine nature. The living and personal to which her care extends is a concrete whole and is protected and encouraged as a totality.... She aspires to this totality in herself and in others" (*Essays on Woman*, 45).

And yet, are there feminine vocations other than the *natural* one?

"Only subjective delusion could deny that women are capable of practicing vocations other than that of spouse and mother," Edith noted clearly. In case of need, "every normal and healthy woman is able to hold a position. And there is no profession which cannot be practiced by a woman. A self-sacrificing woman can accomplish astounding achievements when it is a question of replacing the breadwinner of fatherless children, of supporting abandoned children or aged parents," she added. Like a man, each woman has "her individual specialty and talent, and this talent gives her the capability of doing professional work, be it artistic, scientific, technical, etc. Essentially, the individual talent can enable her to embark on any discipline, even those remote from the usual feminine vocations.... Basically the same spiritual attitude which the wife and mother need is needed here also, except that it is extended to a wider working circle and mostly to a changing area of people; for that reason, the perspective is detached from the vital bond of blood relationship and more highly elevated on the spiritual level" (ibid., 49).

One can say, Edith observed, that "the professions whose objective requirements are not harmonious with feminine nature, those termed as specifically masculine, could yet be practiced in an authentically feminine way if accepted as part of the concrete human condition.... The development of the feminine nature can become a blessed counterbalance precisely here where everyone is in danger of becoming mechanized and losing his humanity. This," Edith added, "is a way for professional life to be formed by the feminine characteristic.... Thus the participation of women in the most diverse professional disciplines could be a blessing for the entire society, private or public, precisely if the specifically feminine ethos would be preserved" (ibid., 51).

Every woman is meant to develop this common sense of spiritual mothering, of companion and mother, in order to help others develop to their fullest potential. "The body of woman is fashioned 'to be one flesh' with another and to nurse new human life in itself," Edith emphasized. "A well disciplined body is an accommodating instrument for the mind which animates it; at the same time, it is a source of power and a habitat for the mind. Just so, woman's soul is designed to be subordinate to man in obedience and support; it is also fashioned to be a shelter in which other souls may unfold. Both spiritual companionship and spiritual motherliness are not limited to the physical spouse and mother relationships, but they extend to all people with whom woman comes into contact" (ibid., 132). Seeing motherhood as a universal calling for all women means it is not simply a duty to be exercised with one's biological children. In Edith's exposition, a woman's concern for the good of persons must be universal, extending to all whose lives touch hers in some way.

"The soul of woman must therefore be *expansive* and open to all human beings," Stein wrote of this spiritual maternity to all people; "it must be *quiet*, so that no small weak flame will be extinguished by stormy winds; warm so as not to benumb fragile buds; *clear*, so that no vermin will settle in dark corners and recesses; *self-contained*, so that no invasions from without can imperil the inner life; *empty of itself*, in order that extraneous life may have room in it; finally, *mistress of itself* and also of its body, so that the entire person is readily at the disposal of every call" (ibid., 132–133).

Ultimately, Edith believed that a "wholesome collaboration of the sexes" in professional life is possible only if both achieve "a calm and objective awareness of their nature and draw practical conclusions from it. God created humanity as man and woman, and He created both according to His own image. Only the purely developed masculine and feminine nature can yield the highest attainable likeness to God. Only in this fashion can there be brought about the strongest interpenetration of all earthly and divine life" (ibid., 57).

Edith finds the ultimate and ideal model of authentic feminism in the Blessed Virgin Mary. "That is an ideal image of the gestalt of the feminine soul. The soul of the first woman was formed for this purpose, and so, too, was the soul of the Mother of God. In all other women since the Fall, there is an embryo of such development, but it needs particular motivation if it is not to be suffocated among weeds rankly shooting up around it." While the religious vocation offers a "supernatural vocation," which comes from God, ultimately, "whether she is a mother in the home, or occupies a place in the limelight of public life, or lives behind quiet cloister walls, she must be a handmaid of the Lord everywhere. So had the Mother of God been in all circumstances of her life, as the Temple virgin enclosed in that hallowed precinct, by her quiet work in Bethlehem and Nazareth, as guide to the apostles and the Christian community after the death of her son. Were each woman an image of the Mother of God, a Spouse of Christ, an apostle of the divine Heart, then would each fulfill her feminine vocation no matter what conditions she lived in and what worldly activity absorbed her life" (ibid., 133, 53–54).

Since the Mother of God is among women "the most intimately bound to Christ," reasons Edith in words that shadow her earlier philosophical reflections on empathy, "she is the heart of the Church of which Christ is the head." Mary helps "those who strive to unveil Christ in the heart of another. Thus, woman's mission is to imitate Mary. She must further the life of faith by providing secure and enduring foundation. As teacher, she must be the maternal, loving educator for Christ. She must nourish a rich life of faith in young persons through their intellectuality and voluntariness. By so consecrating herself to supernatural maternity, the Catholic woman becomes an organ of the Church. And, in this way, she will fulfill this function in the religious life as in a life united to God in the world" (ibid., 36).

Chapter 11

⁓

Catholic Circles: Writing as Political Stance

Scholars have long sought to classify Edith's extensive writings
by various measuring sticks: by set stages of her life (philosopher,
translator/popularizer, theologian); by major personal milestones
(her baptism, entrance into Carmel); by the genre of her writing
(philosophy, theology, devotional, personal essays); even by her
intended audience (women, philosophers, Catholic educators).
But while is it obvious that her writing, as a body, is both impressive and extensive, it remains hard to fit within any particular
label. Edith wrote both anonymous and autographed works. She
wrote book reviews and published her lectures as well as chapters
of her dissertation. She wrote essays and an autobiographical account. She wrote meditations and hagiographies, biographies of
the saints. Throughout her life, Edith wrote plays, skits, and poems.
And she was a prolific and devoted letter writer, with much of the
correspondence still preserved today — in spite of the vast destruction left behind by the Second World War. Writing was intrinsic
to Edith as a person, as a professional, and as a spiritual woman.

In *Writing as Resistance: Four Women Confronting* the *Holocaust*, Rachel Feldhay Brenner presents the life and work of four
Jewish women: Edith Stein, Simone Weil, Anne Frank, and

Edith Stein: St. Teresa Benedicta of the Cross

Etty Hillesum. While facing honestly the reality of their own impending physical destruction as decreed by the "Final Solution," argues Brenner, these four women turned to writing—in the form of diaries, letters, memoirs—as their instruments for making things right in a world that ceased to care for them. As Edith herself noted at the beginning of her family's biography, "Recent months have catapulted the German Jew out of the peaceful existence they had come to take for granted. They have been forced to reflect upon themselves, upon their being, and their destiny.... I was urged to write down what I, child of a Jewish family, had learned about the Jewish people since such knowledge is so rarely found in outsiders," she wrote in 1933. As Germany's "national revolution opened the battle on Judaism, I would like to give, simply, a straightforward account of my own experience of Jewish life as one testimony to be placed alongside others ... as information for anyone wishing to pursue an unprejudiced study from original sources" (*Life*, 23–24).

Even before the official outbreak of Nazi terror, in a world that gave her few options as a woman and as a Jew, Edith utilized writing as a form of intellectual resistance through the power of the pen. Her writing "signified an intellectual and spiritual quest for the moral redemption of the world. The act of writing thus gave (her) a measure of control in a situation where what had seemed immutable ideals and beliefs were in a state of total collapse.... It was the struggle to preserve faith in the reality of a faithless world, to continue to love the world despite its lovelessness, that infused meaning [into the life of Edith Stein]."[22]

---

[22] Rachel Feldhay Brenner, *Writing as Resistance: Four Women Confronting the Holocaust* (University Park, PA: Pennsylvania State University Press, 1997), 9, 10.

Catholic Circles: Writing as Political Stance

For Edith and these three other Jewish women, "preoccupation with the moral condition of a world bent on their destruction demonstrates a remarkable sense of responsibility for the destiny of humanity at large.... All four knew that their ethnic origins turned them into the primary victims of the Nazi terror. Declared Jewish, these assimilated women contended with an identity they did not know, as well as with the terrible and inescapable implications of this identity.... The main purpose of the writings of these four women was not to indict or accuse, and they were not motivated by a desire to avenge through a documented indictment. Rather, their writing was guided ... by their persistent faith in the ethics of the humanistic ideal" (Brenner, *Writing*, 9, 8).

One of Edith's most remarkable body of documents is her legacy of letters to friends, former colleagues, fellow religious, and family members. In spite of the fact that her Carmelite Sisters felt forced to destroy much of Edith's correspondence out of fear that it may harm her or the other Carmelite Sisters if her letters were found by the Nazis, there is still a large collection of her letters left, much of it now collected and translated into English. While, unquestionably, as it was her nature, Edith remained private about explaining the "why" behind much of her life —especially with regards to her conversion—her letters provide a uniquely personal and intimate glimpse into her heart and mind. These letters also help define and present her philosophy as a Catholic scholar.

For Edith, letters provided the opportunity for a "lively exchange of thoughts" with others, and as such, the range of themes is broad. Some of the most significant themes found in her letters include "discussions of philosophical problems and the issue of personal intellectual creativity; pedagogical tasks and the vocation to religious education and leadership; information on the professional life and reflections on a contemplative lifestyle; critique of others and of herself in various situations; religious self-reflection and surrender in religious life; tragic conflict between filial love and witness to God, but a non-conflictual blending of Jewish and Catholic love of God; bonds with home and loving concern for the family in the diaspora; varied, friendly relations and encounters with authorities; dispute with the shocking political situation of the 20th century and recognition of [her] own destiny; life's optimism and resignation" (*Self-Portrait*, xiii).

It is precisely in this writing form that, for her, "questions arise from the hidden depths of the spiritual and emotional life," pointed out Stein scholar Dr. L. Gelber, editor of the printed collection of Edith's letters, *Self-Portrait in Letters: 1916–1942*. "Edith Stein possessed a talent for letter-writing. Her letters reveal a particular lively trait of her personality: while apparently secluded and reticent, she established a sympathetic, close, intellectual and spiritual relationship with like-minded friends" (ibid., xiii). In Edith's own words, "The formation of an unshakable bond with all whom life brings in my way, a bond in no way dependent on day-to-day contact, is a significant element in my life" (ibid., 46). It was a bond that transcended one's stage in life, geography, gender, age, or even religious belief.

To her friend Fritz Kaufmann, who had become estranged from Edith following her conversion to Catholicism, Edith writes with endearing honesty, "A few weeks ago I heard that you almost came to Conrads' in Bergzabern, and yesterday, while putting old letters in order, I came across several of yours. These—I cannot say 'reminded me of you' since forgetting has never been my thing where human relations are concerned—but [the letters] moved you out from the fog-shrouded distance into palpable nearness again, and I wanted to tell you that…. Of course, I would be interested in all you would have to tell me about yourself. But if you prefer not to do so, then just let it be, please. I have always readily understood why you no longer wrote, and have never been cross about it" (ibid., 45–46).

Her letters, especially in her later years, often ended in a personal statement that transcended the formal or the proper. She would often sign, "In His love, your Edith"; "*In Corde Jesu*, your Teresa Benedicta a Cruce"; "In *expectatione Sancti Spiritus*" (in expectation of the Holy Spirit); "From your least" (usually to a fellow religious); or "In the love of the Divine Heart." Her communications reflected her desire to be present to all her correspondents as a faithful and honest friend, and often centered on the reminder to trust in the providence of God—in spite of the hopeless situation that continued to envelop her, her people, and her world.

From her correspondence with Roman Ingarden and with former student Amelie Jaegerschmid—who later became Sister Adelgundis, a member of the Benedictine religious community at St. Lioba's convent in Günterstal—we also learn that amiable contact with her former master, Edmund Husserl, was still significant to Edith. "Four years after her Baptism, she visited Husserl in Freiburg. Both his reception of Edith and their conversation that day were marked with a depth and beauty that she never forgot," wrote the editor of *Life in a Jewish Family*. "It occasioned, however, reflection on her part about the attitude to be taken toward others who do not share one's beliefs. Edith wrote to Sr. Adelgundis in February, 1930, advising her to exercise care when discussing matters of religion, including the last things, with the ailing Husserl" (*Life*, 422).

Edith Stein: St. Teresa Benedicta of the Cross

In this same letter to her former philosophy student, Edith writes that when an encounter with another person "sharpens her awareness, in her own words, 'of our powerlessness to exert a direct influence, I have a deeper sense of the urgency of my own *holocaustum*.' The remembrance of Nazi infamy will always be associated with the name 'Holocaust,'" the editor remarked in a follow-up chronology to *Life in a Jewish Family*; "but for Edith, twelve years before she died during that reign of terror, the word was a challenge to be generous in her everyday life, not only at some moment of extraordinary heroism" (ibid., 422–423).

For eight years at Speyer, Edith studied the intellectual foundation of Catholicism and turned to the philosophy of Thomas Aquinas. According to Stein biographer Dr. Freda Mary Oben, Canon Josef Schwind of the cathedral in Speyer became Stein's revered spiritual director. "He said of Edith laughingly one day that all she wanted to do was talk theology and more theology: theology was her spiritual food! He introduced her to the Jesuit philosopher-theologian Erich Przywara, at whose suggestion she translated into German Cardinal Newman's *Letters and Journals* (1801–1845) and St. Thomas Aquinas' *De Veritate* (On Truth). This was the first adequate translation into German of Aquinas' text. Her two-volume edition of it made her famous, for it was a brilliant phenomenological commentary as well as a translation" (*Edith Stein*, 20).

After Monsignor Schwind died in 1927, he was succeeded as her spiritual director by the archabbot of Beuron, Dom Raphael Walzer, whom Edith considered her religious superior because of the private vows she had taken five years earlier. Aware of Edith's gifts as a philosopher, the Benedictine archabbot encouraged her to participate in international symposia with other well-known and prominent Catholics.

Catholic Circles: Writing as Political Stance

As a broadly educated woman, Edith Stein was a multifaceted speaker and soon became a much-sought-after lecturer throughout German-speaking Europe—in Switzerland, Austria, and Germany in particular—talking to Catholic groups on the education and role of Catholic women and on spirituality. She frequently put herself at the disposal of large Catholic organizations—teachers' associations, women's groups, academic organizations. In 1930, for example, Edith gave a presentation in Salzburg titled "The Ethos of Woman's Vocations." She was the only woman speaking at the large general convention of Catholic Academic Associations.

"Our knowledge is piecemeal. When our will and action build on it alone, they cannot achieve a perfect structure," Edith said at one of her lectures, this one titled "The Spirit of St. Elizabeth as It Informed Her Life." "Nor can that knowledge, because it does not have complete power over the self and often collapses before reaching the goal. And so this inner shaping power that is in bondage strains toward a light that will guide more surely, and a power that will free it and give it space. This is the light and the power of divine grace" (*Hidden Life*, 28).

Although Edith notes that there are "few saints as humanly near to us as our Holy Mother," the words she wrote as a postulant about her Holy Mother Teresa of Avila in a manuscript titled "Love for Love: Life and Works of St. Teresa of Jesus" echo the effect that Edith's life and work were already having on her world: "In incomparably clear, simple and sincere language they tell of the wonders of grace that God worked in a chosen soul. They tell of the indefatigable efforts of a woman with the daring and strength of a man, revealing natural intelligence and heavenly wisdom, a deep knowledge of human nature and a rich spirit's innate sense of humor, the infinite love of a heart tender as a bride's and kind as a mother's." Truly, along with her beloved

Teresa, Edith was walking "the way of perfection hand in hand with her to its goal" (ibid., 65–66).

Edith's final two years as a professional, 1931 and 1932, were some of the busiest of her career. After eight years as a schoolteacher in Speyer, Edith gave up her teaching position to complete her long work, *Potency and Act*, and to enable her to continue to fulfill her many demands as a speaker. Edith traveled to France, Switzerland, and Austria. She continued to speak on education, social justice, women's role in the Church, and personal responsibility.

Without a doubt, her contribution as a philosopher and as a Catholic scholar helped shape Catholic culture in her time and — through the now published collections of her speeches — continues to shape contemporary Catholic thought. In January 1931, Edith once again made attempts to obtain a professorship, this time in Freiburg and at Kiel — both of which were rejected. Eventually, Edith returned to Breslau. In 1932, she was finally offered a post to teach philosophy at the German Institute for Scientific Pedagogy in Münster, where she moved that February.

With a steadily mounting electoral strength, the Nazis had become the second largest party in the country by the 1930 election. On February 25, 1932, Adolf Hitler was granted German citizenship. That same year, Hitler opposed Paul von Hindenburg in Germany's presidential election and captured 36.8 percent of the votes on the second ballot.

Part 4

Blessed by the Truth

Chapter 12

⌒

At Carmel's Door

In 1932, Edith went to Münster, Westphalia, to teach at the German Institute for Scientific Pedagogy, a Catholic institution. She lived under the care of the Sisters of Our Lady at the Collegium Marianum, along with a small group of women students and a large number of nuns who were students, belonging to diverse orders.

Much happened during the two semesters that Edith worked in Münster. On January 30, 1933, Adolf Hitler was appointed chancellor of Germany. Less than two months later, the first concentration camp opened, in Dachau, a German town near Munich. That same year, the Gestapo, the German secret police, was officially established — and anti-Semitic laws ordered Jewish workers in all professions to retire or leave. All Jewish employees of the state, including those who held teaching positions, were dismissed.

It was no different for Edith Stein. In April of 1933, the administrator of the institute where she was teaching told Edith that "he considered it best if I would refrain from scheduling any lectures for [that] summer and just do some quiet research in the Marianum. By autumn the situation would settle down, perhaps the Church would take over the Institute. In that case nothing would prevent me from resuming my activities. I accepted this information very calmly," Edith wrote in her autobiographical sketch, "How I Came to the Cologne Carmel." "I attached no importance to the hopes he held out" (*Selected Writings*, 18).

Edith, who already saw herself as "a stranger in the outside world," believed that the walls that had stood between her and Carmel had now crumbled. She could no longer live out her work as a Catholic laywoman in a secular and increasingly hostile world. "Might not now the time be ripe to enter Carmel?" she wondered. "For almost twelve years, Carmel had been my goal; since summer 1921, when the Life of our Holy Mother Teresa had happened to fall into my hands and had put an end to my long search for the true faith." At the advice of her spiritual adviser and with the awareness that her mother "would not be able to withstand this second blow [after her baptism into the Catholic faith]," Edith had decided to wait patiently. But lately, she acknowledged, "this waiting had become very hard for me" (ibid., 19).

By the end of April, assured within her heart that the time was right, Edith began to take the first steps in preparation. She asked Archabbot Walzer's permission to seek admission to the Carmelite Order, which he granted in mid-May of 1933. Edith then requested that her friend Dr. Elisabeth Cosack arrange an appointment with the Discalced Carmelite nuns in Cologne. On May 20, Edith received an invitation to meet the Mother Prioress in person, an invitation that Edith accepted the same day. As she waited in the chapel for her interview with the Prioress, kneeling close to the altar of Carmelite Thérèse of Lisieux, Edith writes that she "experienced the serenity of someone who has reached her goal." She had worked with Dominicans and admired the Benedictines, yet "it always seemed to me," Edith told the Prioress at Cologne, "that the Lord was saving something for me in Carmel which I could find there and nowhere else" (ibid., 20–21).

On June 19, 1933, Edith was accepted for admission into the Carmel Maria vom Frieden (Mary of Peace) of Cologne-Lindenthal. She spent the month between July 16 and August 15 in the convent's extern quarters, becoming acquainted with the nuns' *horarium*, or daily schedule, and preparing herself for her final visit with her family. Two months later, Edith was admitted into the Cologne Carmel enclosure—on October 14, 1933, the eve of the feast of her beloved spiritual mother, St. Teresa of Avila.

Chapter 13

⁕

Out of Death, New Life

To her Jewish family's shock, Edith entered the Discalced Carmelites in 1933, taking on the name of Sister Teresia Benedicta a Cruce, Latin for "Teresa, blessed by the Cross."

In many respects, following her heart and the certainty with which she felt called to monastic life was easy compared with facing her family—especially her eighty-four-year-old mother. Even through the eighteen months during which Edith negotiated and discussed with the Cologne convent her admittance, she had written to her family only that she had "found a place to stay in Cologne with a group of nuns and would move there for good in October. They wished me good luck as one would for a new job" (*Selected Writings*, 23).

The fact that Edith maintained close ties with her family members, including her eleven nieces and nephews, must have made the task of sharing this formidable change in her life all the more difficult. "I have no doubt that Aunt Edith, who had no children of her own, felt real affection for her nephews and nieces and took an interest in their lives," wrote her niece, who remembered Edith's visits to Breslau. During those visits, Tante

Edith Stein: St. Teresa Benedicta of the Cross

Edith "would appear with a quiet smile and a welcoming word. Those occasions were prized by us [her nieces and nephews], and we recall such precious moments even today.... In her exchange of letters with me, she always responded with sympathetic interest to my concerns and worries." This personal response to her family members continued, even after Edith entered the cloister. "Her letters would at times mention that it was too bad that I could not drop in to visit her in the cloistered serenity of her Carmelite home; I might find peace and healing there" (*Aunt Edith*, 126–127).

That August, Edith finally undertook the "difficult journey" to Breslau to tell her mother and her family her plans in person. She stayed with them for several weeks, as was her custom for her visits in between school semesters. "My mother suffered greatly under the political conditions. She became upset again and again over the fact that 'there are such wicked people in the world,'" Edith wrote. Still, "she revived when I came. Her cheerfulness and her humor came through once again" (*Selected Writings*, 24).

Edith first confided about her decision to enter Carmel in her sister Rosa, who "felt herself a part of the Church ... and was in full agreement with me." Rosa "showed no surprise, and yet," Edith observed, "I noticed that not even she had had an inkling of it." Telling Erna, however, to whom Edith remained very close, was much harder. Edith waited to break the news until her sister asked about the situation in Cologne. "When I answered, she grew pale, and there were tears in her eyes. 'How dreadful life is!' she said. 'What makes one person happy is for another the worst blow imaginable.' She did not try to dissuade me" (ibid., 24–25).

Finally, Edith faced the hardest task of all.

Out of Death, New Life

On the first Sunday in September, my mother and I
were alone in the house. She was sitting at the window
knitting a sock. I sat close by. All of a sudden came the
long-expected question:

"What will you do with the Sisters in Cologne?"

"Live with them."

Now there followed a desperate denial. My mother
never stopped knitting. Her yarn became tangled; with
trembling hands she sought to unravel it, and I helped
her as our discussion continued.

From that time on, Edith wrote, "all tranquility had vanished. A
cloud lay upon the entire household." Various family members,
whether observant Jews or not, tried to influence and dissuade
Edith regarding her decision. Her brother-in-law confronted
Edith, even though he saw no hope for success. "What I was
planning appeared to him to draw the line between myself and
the Jewish people more sharply than before, and that just now,
when they were so sorely oppressed" (ibid., 26).

For her part, Edith realized that scientific objectivity was not
an issue. "The decision was so difficult that no one could tell me
with certainty which was the right path. Good reasons could be
cited for both alternatives. I had to take that step in the complete
darkness of faith" (ibid., 27).

As her day of departure drew closer, many visitors came to
say good-bye—brothers and sisters, their children, her women
friends. On her last day home, when Edith and her mother were
left alone, Edith found the strength to comfort her mourning
mother, whom she so wanted to love and please. Her description of that moment is rich with emotion that transcends and
overflows into the words, in spite of Edith's customary detached-
observer style of writing.

Edith Stein: St. Teresa Benedicta of the Cross

"She covered her face with her hands and began to weep. I stood behind her chair and held her silvery head to my breast. Thus we remained for a long while, until she let me persuade her to go to bed. I took her upstairs and helped her undress, for the first time in my life. Then I sat on the edge of her bed till she herself sent me to bed.... I don't think either of us found any rest that night" (*Selected Writings*, 28).

On Edith's final day in Breslau, her mother began to cry as she did the previous night. She embraced her youngest child and kissed her warmly, weeping aloud. Edith's sister Else clung to her at the train station. It struck Edith that Rosa, by contrast, "was so serene as if she were going along into the tranquility of the convent. Else on the other hand, in her grief suddenly resembled an old woman." As the train left the station, Edith somberly recalled, "I could not feel any wild joy. The scene I had just left behind was too terrible for that. But I felt a deep peace, in the harbor of the divine will." The following day at the Cologne Carmel, "in deep peace I crossed the threshold into the House of the Lord" (ibid., 29, 30).

For the Stein family, Edith's entry into the convent came at the worst possible time. Christianity was, after all, the proclaimed religion of their oppressors, and they could not understand what it meant to Edith or how she could in any way allow herself to be associated with such a religion. Susanne Batzdorff remembers: "At home I had been overhearing my parents talking about it, worrying about how it would affect Grandmother, what it meant for the family, whether Edith's decision was indeed irrevocable or whether she might be dissuaded from her plan. I sensed the gravity of her step, but I understood only how deeply hurt everyone was by it and how we all wished she could be made to change her mind" (*Aunt Edith*, 24). In a newspaper article prior to Edith's beatification, Batzdorff remarked, "She could not have picked a worse time to distance herself from us as Jews, the newly desig-nated pariahs of German society.... Christianity, which Edith had chosen to embrace, was in our eyes in 1933 the religion of our persecutors. For Grandmother Stein, it was the severest blow imaginable. Her daughter Edith was about to enter a cloister in Cologne, a contemplative order with strict rules. She would not be allowed to come home for a visit, ever, and though she could receive visitors, her 84-year-old mother, who had given up all traveling, would never see her again" (*Selected Writings*, 108).

Edith's sister Erna wrote years later that, when Edith traveled to Breslau for the last time that year, "again, I was her confidante, to whom she first communicated her decision to enter the Car-melite Order in Cologne. The weeks that followed were very difficult for us all. My mother was truly in despair and never got over her grief. For the rest of us, too, the farewell this time cut much deeper, although Edith herself did not want to admit it, and even from the convent continued to take part in everything with steadfast love and family loyalty and with undiminished concern" (*Life*, 18).

Edith's family biography, which she began writing while vis-iting her mother and family in Breslau, was—and still is—a source of hurt for Edith's family. Batzdorff quotes a letter (dated November 15, 1997) sent to her by her cousin Lotte Sachs, the youngest daughter of Edith's brother Arno: "I'm just rereading *Aus dem Leben einer jüdischen Familie* (*Life in a Jewish Family*); my reaction to some of the passages is much stronger now than it was when I read the draft in German years ago ... and later the English edition. It seems incredible to me now that Aunt Edith wrote about all the 'warts' of the family in such a direct way; even though the book wasn't published till after the siblings' passing, we, the next generation, might still be suffering" (*Aunt Edith*, 78). Batzdorff also quotes a letter (dated March 5, 1988) from her cousin Anni, one of Else's children, who resented Edith's detailed account of Else's marital problems during the early years of her marriage: "[The book] contains too many things which do not concern the public and can be seen one-sidedly. In my English translation (*Life in a Jewish Family*), I have inserted slips with data which I myself remember, and with corrections (for my family)" (*Aunt Edith*, 80).

Erna's daughter Susanne, who was a newborn when Tante Edith was baptized, also remembers the last conversation she had with her aunt shortly before Edith's departure for the Cologne Carmel. As they walked home from the dentist's office together, then-twelve-year-old Susanne asked Edith her "burning question, 'Tante Edith, why are you doing this? Why are you doing this—now?' My aunt with her quiet smile, her severe hairstyle, her dimpled chin, bowed slightly to come closer to her little niece, to try to answer a difficult question. Why? And why now? She must have grasped instantly what lay hidden behind my brief, anguished outburst," Batzdorff wrote in *Aunt Edith*. "'Susel, listen to me. I am becoming a Carmelite, because I must follow my conscience. But that does not mean that I am abandoning you. I will always be part of this family, I will always love you and take an interest in you. I'll write to you and I'll want to hear from you.' I heard her words, but I felt our relationship could not be as before. I had no words to express my sadness, my doubts, my lack of hope.... [Now], sixty-five years later, I am still trying to understand" (ibid., 24–25).

Batzdorff expresses her own feelings and expands on her memories of her aunt Edith, small in physical stature but tall in personal influence, in a poem titled "Tante Edith," published in her book (ibid., 26–27).

Out of Death, New Life

A firm handshake,
A cloud-soft voice,
A gentle smile,
But cool, aloof.

Your nephews bow,
The nieces curtsy,
A bit in awe
Minding their manners.

This special aunt
Makes appearances
Only rarely, no more
Than twice a year.

Tante Edith had dimples
In her chin.
Her soft brown hair
Is combed straight back,
A bit too severely.
Are you afraid
To let any wisps
Or curls escape
From the straight and narrow?

In that long-ago time
You kept us at arm's length.
Your time was precious.
You were always writing
Or seeing visitors.
We remained outside
The heavy doors, which

Edith Stein: St. Teresa Benedicta of the Cross

Kept your voices muffled,
Strictly confidential.

Oh, Tante Edith,
We hardly knew you.
Who are you, really?
A mix of theology
And phenomenology?
Of Jewish ancestors
And priestly mentors?

A follower after
Strange gods?
[What] led you to worship
The Jew on the cross?

Grandmother's favorite,
My mother's playmate.
How do you fit
Into my family?
Where do you belong?

You puzzled your brothers
And sisters,
When you took the veil
Of Carmel.

Grandmother shook her head
And shed silent tears.
Her whole body shook
With soundless weeping
The day you left
To become a nun.

Chapter 14

⌐

Fullness of Faith: Edith the Contemplative

Although she had obvious ties with the Dominicans and the Benedictines, Edith's heart was with Carmel. In addition to Teresa of Avila, to whom Edith credited her Catholic faith, surely she must have also felt at home with the Israeli origins of the Carmelite Order as well as the community's traditional devotion to Elijah, whom the order calls its father and model.

Mentioned often in Old Testament writings, Carmel, a sacred mountain just south of the Israeli city of Haifa, overlooks the city's harbor and the Mediterranean Sea. Toward the end of the twelfth century, a group of hermits settled on the western slopes of Mount Carmel, desiring to imitate Elijah the prophet by living a hermitlike life in the grottoes of the mountain where Elijah was said to have lived.

The Carmelites honor Elijah as a great prophet through whom was made manifest, on the very summit of the holy mountain, the power of the true God. As Edith herself describes in her essay "On the History and Spirit of Carmel," "We who live in Carmel and who daily call on our Holy Father Elijah in prayer know that for us he is not a shadowy figure out of the dim past. His spirit is active among us in a vital tradition and determines how we live." Indeed, to stand before the face of the living God, as Elijah did (see 1 Kings 17), says Edith, "that is our vocation. The holy prophet set us an example. He stood before God's face because this was the eternal treasure for whose sake he gave up all earthly goods.... He is for us an example of the gospel poverty that we have vowed, an authentic prototype of the Savior" (*Hidden Life*, 1–2).

Edith took to heart the history and charisma of the order, including the life and example of St. Thérèse of Lisieux, a fellow Carmelite and semicontemporary of Edith, having died in 1897, when Edith was a young child of six. "St. Thérèse of the Child Jesus shows you even in the little details of daily life how one can follow him and Mary in Carmel," Edith wrote years later on the occasion of the first profession of one of the novices. "If you learn from her to depend on God alone and serve him with a wholly pure and detached heart, then you can join with your whole soul in singing the jubilant song of the holy Virgin, 'My soul proclaims the greatness of the Lord, and my spirit rejoices in God my Savior. For he has done great things for me, and holy is his name.' And like little St. Thérèse you will be able to say at the end, 'I do not regret that I have given myself to love'" (ibid., 108).

Coincidentally, Edith shared a trait uniquely personal with the best-known Carmelite saints — Teresa of Avila, John of the Cross, and Thérèse of Lisieux. Each of them, like Edith, lost a parent when they were still children. Teresa was thirteen years old when she lost her mother; Thérèse was four. And John of the Cross was an infant when his father died. As biographers tell us, each of these Carmelite saints had a strong and caring surviving parent to guide them.

Edith was accepted as a Carmelite novice on April 15, 1934. With the words of Elijah — which make up the motto on the shield of the Carmelite Order — Edith, too, could now proclaim, "with zeal be zealous for the Lord, the God of Hosts." Along with the Discalced Carmelite habit, Edith took on the name of Sister Teresia Benedicta a Cruce. "By the cross, I understood the fate of the people of God," she wrote later, "which was then already beginning to be proclaimed." Two years before her arrest and death, Edith proclaimed, "After all, one cannot wish for a deliverance from the Cross when one bears the noble title 'of the Cross'" (*Self-Portrait*, 327).

In her essay "Love of the Cross: Some Thoughts for the Feast of St. John of the Cross," Edith wrote about her devotion to the Cross, "The burden of the cross that Christ assumed is that of corrupted human nature, with all its consequences in sin and suffering to which fallen humanity is subject. The meaning of the way of the cross is to carry this burden out of the world. . . . The lovers of the cross whom he has awakened and will always continue to awaken anew in the changeable history of the struggling church, these are his allies at the end of time. We, too, are called for that purpose." When someone "desires to suffer," it is not merely a pious reminder of the suffering of the Lord; it truly unites one to the Lord intimately, Edith explained in this meditation, written presumably in 1934, after her entrance into the Carmel of Cologne. "Only someone whose spiritual eyes have been opened to the supernatural correlations of worldly events can desire suffering in expiation, and this is only possible for people in whom the spirit of Christ dwells, who as members [*Glieder*] are given life by the Head, receive his power, his meaning, and his direction." Ultimately, she emphasized, "because *being* one with Christ is our sanctity, and progressively *becoming* one with him our happiness on earth, the love of the cross in no way contradicts being a joyful child of God. Helping Christ carry his cross fills one with a strong and pure joy, and those who may and can do so, the builders of God's kingdom, are the most authentic children of God" (*Hidden Life*, 91–93).

On August 2, 1934, Paul von Hindenburg, the president of Germany, died, and Adolf Hitler became president and commander-in-chief of the armed forces. Six months later, Hitler rejected the Treaty of Versailles and began to draft Germans into military service. By the end of 1935, the Nuremberg Laws denied Jews citizenship in Germany. And the Nazi symbol, a black swastika — an ancient religious sign formed from a Greek cross — within a round white field on red cloth, became the official German flag.

During her novitiate year, Edith returned to writing, in obedience to her provincial's wishes. She completed the index for her translation of St. Thomas and contributed to a number of periodicals. All who enter Carmel, Edith wrote, "must give themselves wholly to the Lord. Only one who values her little place in the choir before the tabernacle more highly than all the splendor of the world can live here, can then truly find a joy that no worldly splendor has to offer" (*Hidden Life*, 6).

On April 21, 1935, Edith took her first vows. "Carmelites can repay God's love by their everyday lives in no other way than by carrying out their daily duties faithfully in every respect.... This is the 'little way,' a bouquet of insignificant little blossoms that are daily placed before the Almighty — perhaps a silent, life-long martyrdom that no one suspects and that is at the same time a source of deep peace and hearty joyousness and a fountain of grace that bubbles over everything — we do not know where it goes, and the people whom it reaches do not know from whence it comes" (ibid., 6).

Edith, in fact, yearned to devote herself to a complete life of prayer. But instead, she was asked by her Prioress to finish the philosophical work that she had begun in Speyer, *Potency and Act*, which combined phenomenology and Catholic tradition. Edith was determined to do her best. As Carmelite biographer Sister Waltraud Herbstrith noted, "It ended up taking all her hard-won self-discipline to learn how to break her concentration every time the bell was rung. She publicly admitted that she found it her severest penance. When Sunday came, her serious face would beam and she would say, 'Thank God, I don't have to write today. Today I can pray'" (*Edith Stein*, 134). Edith completed her study *Finite and Eternal Being* in the summer of 1936.

That fall, news arrived that Edith's mother had died of stomach cancer. In the nearly three years between her entry into Carmel in 1933 and her mother's death in September 1936, Edith and her mother never met again. "So deep was Auguste Stein's resentment," remarked Edith's niece Susanne Batzdorff, "that many months went by before she could bring herself to add even a short greeting to a letter which Edith's sisters were sending out to her" (*Aunt Edith*, 85). Edith's mother never wrote personally in the first year Edith spent in Carmel, and eventually added only a few lines at the conclusion of Rosa's letters to Edith. These short lines, however, were of great consolation for Edith, whose intention for her mother continued to be "that all the harshness and bitterness of the past years should disappear, and that peace might come" (*Self-Portrait*, 229).

As her mother's terminal illness progressed, Edith heard from her sisters that Frau Stein was "constantly brooding," wondering why her youngest had "forsaken" her (ibid., 233). "I was never able to make Mother comprehend either my conversion or my entrance into the Order," Edith wrote in a letter two months before her mother's death. "And so, once more, she is suffering greatly because of our separation, and I am unable to say anything that will comfort her" (ibid., 230). Edith, whose letters to friends are full of requests for prayers for the healing of her mother's embitterment, ultimately had to accept Frau Stein's sadness and pain as something that she could not change. "'[We know that for those who love him, God turns everything to the good]' will surely apply to my dear mother, too, since she truly loved 'her' God (as she often said with emphasis). And, with confidence in him, she bore much that was painful and did much that was good.... And no one but the Lord himself knows what is happening in her soul" (ibid., 235), wrote Edith the day before her mother's death—September 14, 1936, the feast of the Holy Cross. Symbolically, September 14 is also the day that the Carmelite nuns annually renewed their vows. Edith said afterward, "'As I was standing in my place in choir waiting to renew my vows my mother was beside me. I felt her presence quite distinctly.' This was believable, given the special bond of love between them and Edith's intuitive power which was now developing in a mystical direction" (Oben, *Edith Stein*, 31).

On October 25, 1936, Hitler and Italian dictator Benito Mussolini signed a treaty, forming the Rome-Berlin Axis.

During her nine years as a Carmelite, Edith continued to write various projects, including the family history that she had started a few years before at the request of one of her priest advisers, in order to give, as she explains clearly in the foreword to her family's history, "a straightforward account of my own experience of Jewish life as one testimony to be placed alongside others ... for anyone wishing to pursue an unprejudiced study from original sources." Edith believed this type of personal account was needed because of the vast number of people in her culture who were "reared in racial hatred from earliest childhood. To all who have been thus deprived, we who grew up in Judaism have an obligation to give our testimony." The result was *Life in a Jewish Family*, a personal account that ends abruptly in 1916, at the moment that Edith completed her examination summa cum laude for her doctor of philosophy degree and agreed to become Husserl's assistant. While we are unable to know for sure the reasons, it is reasonable to assume that Edith could not continue writing her family's history because of the risk involved to the Echt community if the Nazis found such a manuscript—and its author—residing in the convent.

Edith acknowledges in the manuscript's foreword that the idea of writing her family's history came as a suggestion from "a priest belonging to a religious order." Yet the honesty and vulnerability with which she approached the writing of *Life in a Jewish Family* is an example of Edith's desire to live out the meaning and depth inherent in a life of sacrifice and prayer. "She is offering up the enormous fact of her family's reality, its appeal, its humanity, to the hostile gaze of a world lit by racial hatred," writes Patricia Hampl in her essay on Edith Stein. "The Greek root of the word *martyr* is often invoked: It means to witness. But in a deeper recess of the word's etymology there is also a related Sanskrit derivation—from *smar*, to remember. A fierce act of memory then—the will to remember—is the hidden kernel of the martyr's calling. And naturally, the martyr's literary form would be the memoir" (*Stories*, 127).

Her second family, the Carmelites who came to know Edith in the cloister, remember her goodness and her laughter. According to Oben's biographical record of nuns who had lived with Edith, published in 1988, "[Edith's] stories and humor enchanted the nuns, but above all, they were struck by her humility, her modesty. She never referred to her importance in the outside world. And, over and over again," Oben noted, "I have heard that Edith had a special gift for relating to people. She intuitively felt the state of mind of others and knew what they needed and how to encourage them. Her love and goodness were natural. She herself had a need to help other people. I asked if she had shown signs of still being artistically inclined and received an enthusiastic, 'Yes!' She loved plastic sculpture and kept a silver Japanese vase in her cell by the Madonna; she had copies of paintings on cards (Rembrandt was her favorite); she had a great love for music, wrote poetry, and created little plays for the nuns' entertainment. The young lady who had so enjoyed dancing, hiking, boating, tennis, theater, concerts and literature was now content behind the cloistered walls" (*Edith Stein*, 29–30).

From her small room Edith also composed prayers and poems, often to commemorate a special occasion in the life of the community. Some of the handwritten originals are in booklet form, adorned with small pen drawings. Others, penciled originals, are written on very thin paper with typescript on its verso — composed under the stress of war, paper shortage, and perhaps in haste. They are often simple, always honest and from the heart, like the following stanzas from a poem titled "I Will Remain with You" (*Hidden Life*, 135, 137, 139), which was most likely written on her departure from the Cologne Carmel on December 31, 1938.

> You reign at the Father's right hand
> In the kingdom of his eternal glory
> As God's Word from the beginning.
> You reign on the Almighty's throne

Edith the Contemplative

Also in transfigured human form,
Ever since the completion of your work on earth.

I believe this because your word teaches me so,
And because I believe, I know it gives me joy,
And blessed hope blooms forth from it.

For where you are, there also are your own,
Heaven is my glorious homeland,
I share with you the Father's throne.

The Eternal who made all creatures,
Who, thrice holy, encompasses all being,
In addition has a silent, special kingdom of his own.

The innermost chamber of the human soul
Is the Trinity's favorite place to be,
His heavenly throne on earth.

To deliver this heavenly kingdom from the hand of
    the enemy,
The Son of God has come as Son of Man,
He gave his blood as the price of deliverance.

In the heart of Jesus, which was pierced,
The kingdom of heaven and the land of earth are
    bound together.
Here is for us the source of life.

Full of love, you sink your gaze into mine
And bend your ear to my quiet words
And deeply fill my heart with peace.
Your body mysteriously permeates mine
And your soul unites with mine:

Edith Stein: St. Teresa Benedicta of the Cross

I am no longer what once I was.

You come and go, but the seed
That you sowed for future glory, remains behind
Buried in this body of dust.

A luster of heaven remains in the soul,
A deep glow remains in the eyes,
A soaring in the tone of voice.

How wonderful are your gracious wonders!
All we can do is be amazed and stammer and fall silent
Because intellect and words fail.

What is surprising about these prayers and poems, notes biographer Sister Waltraud Herbstrith, is that despite her intellectual ability and extensive education, Edith's works are "uncomplicated and carefree as a child.... What impresses us in these lines is the atmosphere of depth, of peace, of childlike trust in God." Her trust "in God's unfathomable mercy never falters." Her piety, noted the editor of the original German edition of Edith's *Selected Writings*, was nourished by the psalms, by the Eucharist, and by delving into the Passion of Jesus Christ. "Despite all darkness and depression, the light of God, God's love, is finally victorious. That is the triumphant joy which Edith passes along to those who pray with her" (*Selected Writings*, 35).

In a poem set to melody (ibid., 37), Edith paraphrased the following stanzas of Psalm 45:

> 1. A festive song streams from my heart,
>   Which to the King I dedicate
>   My tongue shall take the pen's swift part
>   His praises duly to relate.

He is most glorious to behold
His arm is powerful and bold.

2. The Queen stands ever by His side
In splendid, gold-brocaded gown;
Demure young maidens with her stride
Whom He has raised to high renown.
A joyous chorus, sweet they sing,
Entering the palace of the King.

On Christmas Eve, 1936, three months after the death of their mother, Rosa Stein became a Roman Catholic. Rosa was baptized in the chapel of St. Elizabeth's Hospital in Cologne-Lindenthal. Providentially, Edith was a patient in the surgical ward of this clinic at that time because of an accident on the convent stairs in which she broke her wrist and her foot. This accident allowed Edith to be present at her sister's baptismal ceremony. Rosa, who originally wanted to become an extern Carmelite Sister and join Edith, became instead a Third Order Carmelite and portress (doorkeeper) of the convent at Echt on July 1, 1939. The following poem was written by Edith in remembrance of December 24, 1936, the day Rosa entered the Church. It is titled simply, "For Rosa's Baptism. Holy Night" (ibid., 59).

My Lord, God, You have led me by a long, dark path,
Rocky and hard.
Often my strength threatened to fail me.
I almost lost all hope of seeing the light.
But when my heart grew numb with deepest grief,
A clear star rose for me.
Steadfast it guided me—I followed,
At first reluctant, but more confidently later.

Edith Stein: St. Teresa Benedicta of the Cross

At last I stood at Church's gate.
It opened. I sought admission.
From your priest's mouth Your blessing greets me.
Red blossom stars show me the path to You.
They wait for You at Holy Night.
But Your goodness
Allows them to illuminate my path to You.
They lead me on.
The secret which I had to keep in hiding
Deep in my heart,
Now I can shout it out:
I believe—I profess!
The priest accompanies me to the altar:
I bend my face—
Holy water flows over my head.

Lord, is it possible that someone who is past
Midlife can be reborn?
You said so, and for me it was fulfilled,
A long life's burden of guilt and suffering
Fell away from me.
Erect I receive the white cloak,
Which they place round my shoulders,
Radiant image of purity!
In my hand I hold a candle.
Its flame makes known
That deep within me glows Your holy life.
My heart has become Your manger,
Awaiting You,
But not for long!
Maria, Your mother and also mine,

Has given me her name.
At midnight she will place her newborn child
Into my heart.

Ah, no one's heart can fathom,
What You've in store for those who love You.
Now You are mine, and I won't let You go.
Wherever my life's road may lead,
You are with me.
Nothing can ever part me from Your love.

In March of 1938 Hitler's troops invaded Austria and, six months later, the Sudetenland, sections of northern and western Bohemia and northern Moravia that had a predominantly German population. By a combination of external and internal pressures, Hitler succeeded within months in annexing or neutralizing all of what had been Czechoslovakia. That same year, on April 21, 1938, the Thursday after Easter, Edith Stein made her perpetual vows as a Carmelite, exchanging the white veil she had worn since her days as a novice for the black veil of a Discalced Carmelite nun. A few days later, Edith received notice that her "Master" at Göttingen and Freiburg, Edmund Husserl, had died on April 27.

Much had changed in the outside world in those three years since her first profession. And Edith's spiritual awareness led her to a mystic knowledge of the approaching sacrifices that would be asked of her, even as her faith strengthened. This is Edith's profound experience of the Science of the Cross. "For her the Cross was never some mystery of the faith passively accepted, but a living reality, the seed of which had first been cast into her soul when she met its strength-giving power in the widow of her teacher Reinach, and from then onwards grew until it was also outwardly revealed in her name, Benedicta of the Cross," wrote biographer Hilda Graef. On Good Friday, 1938, Edith wrote a poem, "Iuxta Crucem Tecum Stare!" (loosely translated, "Beneath the Cross I Stood with You!"), dedicated to the Virgin Mary, that reflected what "she knew to be her own vocation," to stand beneath the Cross for the souls entrusted to her care.[23]

> Today I stood with you beneath the Cross,
> And felt more clearly than I ever did
> That you became our Mother only there.
> Even an earthly mother faithfully
> Seeks to fulfill the last will of her son.
> But you became the handmaid of the Lord;
> The life and being of the God made Man
> Was perfectly inscribed in your own life.
> So you could take your own into your heart,
> And with the lifeblood of your bitter pains
> You purchased life anew for every soul.
> You know us all, our wounds, our imperfections;
> But you know also the celestial radiance
> Which your Son's love would shed on us in Heaven.
> Thus carefully you guide our faltering footsteps,
> No price too high for you to lead us to our goal.
> But those whom you have chosen for companions
> To stand with you round the eternal throne,
> They here must stand with you beneath the Cross,
> And with the lifeblood of their bitter pains

[23] Hilda C. Graef, *The Scholar and the Cross: The Life and Work of Edith Stein* (Westminster, MD: Newman Press, 1955), 209–210.

Must purchase heavenly glory for those souls
Whom God's own Son entrusted to their care.

A mere few months later, on November 9, 1938, hundreds of synagogues across Germany and Austria were destroyed in what became known as *Kristallnacht*, the Night of Broken Glass. Thousands of Jewish-owned stores and businesses were broken into and robbed. Jews from all walks of life were collected, arrested, and sent to concentration camps or killed. The Neue Synagoge in Breslau, the formidable structure where Auguste Stein worshipped and where Edith would accompany her on her visits to Breslau, was set afire and destroyed by explosives.

Sources note that, aware of the danger to her Carmel and, indeed, to anyone associated with Jews, Edith requested a transfer to a foreign Carmel, probably in the Holy Land. But the British had already closed that escape route. Edith transferred instead to the Carmelite monastery in Echt, a small town in the Netherlands, on December 31, 1938.

Chapter 15

⁀

The Last Days

"Perhaps I shall leave this house soon after Christmas," Edith wrote from Cologne on December 18, 1938, the fourth Sunday of Advent. "The circumstances which have forced us to initiate my transfer to Echt (Holland) are strikingly reminiscent of the situation at the time of my entrance into the Carmel. It is likely that there is a subtle connection between the two" (*Selected Writings*, 15).

As the Third Reich's ethnic cleansing against the Jews escalated, Edith was transferred from her convent in Cologne to Echt. A passport picture that she had to have taken for her passport has now become an icon of Sister Teresa Benedicta of the Cross. This was the image that appeared on a German postage stamp in 1983 and was enlarged for the gigantic banner that hung above the altar during her 1987 beatification Mass in the Cologne stadium.

Not only did Edith want to hear the truth, even when it was at her own expense, she also had the courage to say it to and about others, stated Jesuit Father Jan H. Nota, who became friends with Stein during her years at Echt. "The fascinating thing to me about Edith Stein was that truth did not exist as an abstraction for her but as something incarnated in persons and therefore as inconceivable apart from love.... The Christ she had encountered as a phenomenologist was the one who had revealed himself within his Church, not some rationalistic projection of him. In the same way, Christ was a Jew, and Edith Stein felt proud to belong to his people" (Herbstrith, *Edith Stein*, 11). As Edith herself said, "If God is within us and if God is love, it cannot be otherwise than that we love our brothers and sisters. Therefore our love of human beings is the measure of our love of God. For the Christian," she proclaimed in her experience of Truth, "there is no such thing as a stranger. At any time it is our neighbor who stands before us, the one who needs us the most; regardless of whether he is related or not, whether we like him or not, whether he is 'morally deserving' or not."[24]

In many respects, the words Edith uses to describe the profound effect that Teresa of Avila, the order's Mother Superior, had on the Church and on her conflicted world, can be applied to Edith and her environment: "It was precisely that she lived in prayer and allowed herself to be drawn ever more deeply by the Lord into the depths of her 'interior castle' until she reached that obscure room where he could say to her, 'that now it was time that she consider as her own what belonged to him, and that he would take care of what was hers.'" As Edith explains, "Whoever surrenders unconditionally to the Lord will be chosen by him as an instrument for building his kingdom" (*Hidden Life*, 14–15).

Official records of history, notes Edith, are simply silent about the "invisible and incalculable forces" of the prayers offered behind monastery walls by those who have devoted their life unconditionally to Christ. This is the hidden life that Edith

[24] *An Edith Stein Daybook: To Live at the Hand of the Lord*, trans. Susanne Batzdorff (Springfield, IL: Templegate, 1994), 116.

sought and proclaimed, the inner world she first became aware of as a young child. "There must be special places on earth for the solemn praise of God, places where this praise is formed into the greatest perfection of which humankind is capable. From such places it can ascend to heaven for the whole church and have an influence on the church's members; it can awaken the interior life in them and make them zealous for external unanimity." But, says Edith about the effects of Teresa's prayers on history—and in words that foreshadow her own influence—"[these interior forces] are recognized by the trust of the faithful and the carefully balanced judgment of the church after extensive investigations. And our time is more and more determined, when all else fails, to hope for ultimate salvation from these hidden sources" (ibid., 14–15). Indeed, days after the official outbreak of World War II, Edith solemnly declared in a letter, "We feel called upon by current events to take our vocation most seriously" (*Self-Portrait*, 312).

In a January 2, 1939, article, *Time* magazine granted Adolf Hitler the title "Man of the Year" for 1938. On January 30, 1939, in a speech before the German parliament, Hitler declared that if war broke out, all the Jews in Europe would be destroyed.

In a letter a few months later—dated March 26, 1939, Passion Sunday—to Mother Ottilia Thannisch, O.C.D., Prioress of the Carmel of Echt at that time, Edith writes, "Dear Mother: please allow me to offer myself to the heart of Jesus as a sacrifice of propitiation for true peace, that the dominion of the Antichrist may collapse, if possible, without a new world war, and that a new order may be established? I would like it (my request) granted this very day because it is the twelfth hour. I know that I am nothing, but Jesus desires it, and surely he will call many others to do likewise in these days" (ibid., 305).

Edith Stein: St. Teresa Benedicta of the Cross

Five months later, Edith wrote to Professor Peter Wust in Münster, not only to assure the sick professor of her prayers, but also to share with him her perspective on suffering. In Edith's typical direct and honest manner, she declares to him: "I was deeply moved that the suffering involves for you the very organs with which so many sins are committed today. It seems to me like a call to make a particular kind of reparation. Such a call is an extraordinary grace. I believe that such suffering, when it is accepted with a willing heart and carried to the end, is reckoned before God as a true martyrdom. It is in this sense that I remember you before the Lord. I beg him for strength also for your dear relatives for whom the sacrifice is surely even harder than for yourself" (ibid., 310–311).

Alert to the fateful and disastrous developments that step by step were unfolding into another world war, Edith's letters, postcards, and cards to friends and former colleagues were full of requests and thanksgiving for prayers on behalf of her family. "For the moment, I can see hardly any (other) possibility than to help by prayer, and so I want to call upon all my auxiliary troops," which in Edith's personal life was nothing short of a regiment of friends. The Stein family "is scattered all over the world," Edith wrote, "but God knows the good of that" (ibid., 301). Even as her sisters, brothers, nieces, and nephews left the continent—for the United States, South America, Norway—Edith remained steadfast in her prayers and requests on their behalf. In a letter dated February 17, 1939, for example, she asked Mother Petra Brüning, O.S.U., in Dorsten for "a Mass for my relatives, living and deceased," explaining, "For my mother, of course, I am wholly confident. But lately I found my soul very burdened at the thought that I have done so very little for my father. He died when I was not quite two years old; I have no memory of my own about him, although my mother always tried her best to evoke memories (in me)" (ibid., 302).

In various letters dated April 1939, Edith writes: "Please continue the prayers; my relatives are still very much in need of them." "I beg you earnestly to continue [your prayers]; I always need them urgently for my dear relatives and for many intentions" (ibid., 305–306). And finally in September, "May I beg you to include my relatives in [your remembrance at the altar] (the family is now very scattered, but in our hearts all the more closely united) and that holds too for the two monastic families of Cologne and Echt, in which I now have the rights of home" (ibid., 311). In her letters Edith also requested of fellow Carmelites that they "commend [her sister Erna] to the Mother of God, that she may lead her to sources of happiness and strength." Edith worried about Erna, who was about to celebrate her fiftieth birthday in New York, "and she is greatly in need of prayers so that she can recover from the great difficulties she has passed through, and catch up on all her duties as wife and mother" (ibid., 317).

"When in February 1939 I followed my husband to America with my children, [Edith] would have liked us to visit her in Echt," Erna remembered years later. "We had booked passage via Hamburg and, since crossing the Dutch border was considered to be particularly troublesome, we did not want to risk it. We kept in touch by mail, and I felt fairly well reassured that, now, in the shelter of the convent she was safe from Hitler's aggression, just like my sister Rosa, who through Edith's intervention had also found refuge in Echt. Sadly this belief proved to be unjustified" (*Life*, 18).

Hitler's hateful invasion did not end when he united Europe's German-speaking peoples. On September 1, 1939, Germany invaded Poland, home to more than three million Jews. Two days later, Great Britain and France declared war on Germany. The Second World War had officially begun.

Edith, in the meantime, remained at peace spiritually, proclaiming in her writing her awareness of God's divine providence. "My basic attitude since I've been here is one of gratitude — grateful that I may be here and that the house is as it is," wrote Edith in a letter to an Ursuline friend from Echt. "At the same time I always have a lively awareness that we do not have a lasting city here (Heb. 13:14). I have no other desire than that God's will be done in me and through me. It is up to him how long he leaves me here and what is to come then. *In manibus tuis sortes meae* (My days are in your hands, Psalm 31:15). There everything is well cared for. I need not worry about anything. But much prayer is necessary in order to remain faithful in all situations" (*Self-Portrait*, 309).

During her three years at Echt, Edith worked closely with the young Carmelite novices, whom she endearingly called "the little ones." Edith had a strong influence on the young Sisters' formation, giving them daily classes in Latin and enlisting them in the presentation of "stage plays," which she often wrote for her spiritual family, much in the same way that as a youth she used to write dramatic and oral pieces to celebrate special occasions for her natural family. In addition to her philosophical writings, Edith's literary talents included essays that she wrote for the Prioress to present as sources of meditation, as well as fictional pieces in dialogue form and poetry.

For September 14, 1939, the feast of the Exaltation of the Cross — and at her Prioress's request — Edith wrote an expressive and challenging meditation for the community's biannual renewal of vows, an occasion she viewed as "dreadfully serious business." "More than ever the cross is a sign of contradiction.

The Last Days

The followers of the Antichrist show it far more dishonor than did the Persians who stole it. They desecrate the images of the cross, and they make every effort to tear the cross out of the hearts of Christians. All too often they have succeeded even with those who, like us, once vowed to bear Christ's cross after him," remarked Edith in a text titled "Elevation of the Cross." "Therefore, the Savior today looks at us, solemnly probing us, and asks each one of us: Will you remain faithful to the Crucified? Consider carefully! The world is in flames, the battle between Christ and the Antichrist has broken into the open. If you decide for Christ, it could cost you your life. Carefully consider what you promise.... The world is in flames. The conflagration can also reach our house. But high above all flames towers the cross. They cannot consume it. It is the path from earth to heaven. It will lift one who embraces it in faith, love, and hope into the bosom of the Trinity" (*Hidden Life*, 94–95).

By the end of 1939, Germany and the Soviets had occupied Estonia, Latvia, and Lithuania and had attacked Finland, which they finally defeated in March 1940. The next month, Germany occupied several Norwegian ports and all of Denmark. On April 27, 1940, orders were issued to set up a concentration camp at Auschwitz, Poland, the first of three at this location. Before the end of the war, more than one hundred concentration camps and a total of six death camps had been set up by the Nazis in various parts of Europe. On May 10, the major German offensive in the West began with a lightning sweep through the Netherlands and Belgium into France. By June 22, three-fifths of France, including Paris, was occupied.

In a letter to Mother Johanna van Weersth of the Beek Carmel, Edith relates a visit to the Sisters by Bishop J.H.G. Lemmens. The bishop, wrote Edith on July 10, 1940, "exhorted us not to worry, to have great confidence, to sleep well, and to talk to one another more frequently since this would be good for us at a time like this. But above all else he urged us, of course, to untiring prayer and sacrifice and to fidelity to our vocation since we must now fight in the front line." Neither Bolshevism nor National Socialism "would be victorious, because in the end Christ would conquer," the bishop assured the nuns. "All of us would at some time have to get on our knees. But first there would be a relentless battle between these philosophies of life. He continued: we had nothing against the people as individuals. But we have to be steadfast in our principles and may not surrender on any point.... [The bishop] will gladly accept being *episcopus et martyr* (bishop and martyr)," Edith concluded the letter (*Self-Portrait*, 324–325).

This time, for the renewal of their vows on September 14, 1940, Edith prepared a meditation for her Prioress titled "The Marriage of the Lamb," in which she examined the "mysterious words" of Revelation 19:7: *For this is the wedding day of the Lamb; his bride has prepared herself for the wedding.* "Just as the Lamb had to be killed to be raised upon the throne of glory," Edith wrote, "so the path to glory leads through suffering and the cross for everyone chosen to attend the marriage supper of the Lamb. All who want to be married to the Lamb must allow themselves to be fastened to the cross with him. Everyone marked by the blood of the Lamb is called to this, and that means all the baptized. But not everyone understands the call and follows it." Edith sets up a distinction between the "children of God" and the "children of this world" in their understanding of freedom. "Children of this world say they are free when they are not subject to another's will, when no one stops them from satisfying their wishes and inclinations. For this dream of freedom, they engage in bloody battles and sacrifice life and limb.

The children of God see freedom as something else. They want to be unhindered in following the Spirit of God; and they know that the greatest hindrances do not come from without, but lie within us ourselves." For those who live a vowed religious life, Edith believed, the "bridal connection with the Savior" is even more prominent. "The bridal happiness and fidelity of the soul consecrated to God must stand the test in open and hidden battles and in the everyday flow of religious life.... If she is to enter into heavenly glory with him, she must allow herself to be fastened to his cross. The three vows are the nails. The more willingly she stretches herself out on the cross and endures the blows of the hammer, the more deeply will she experience the reality of her union with the Crucified. Then being crucified itself becomes for her the marriage feast" (*Hidden Life*, 99).

As she did before, Edith makes a direct reference to the catastrophic events taking place outside the cloister, ending her exhortation with an admonition against the complaint "that the many prayers for peace are still without effect.... The fountain from the heart of the Lamb has not dried up. We can wash our robes clean in it even today as the thief on Golgotha once did. Trusting in the atoning power of this holy fountain, we prostrate ourselves before the throne of the Lamb and answer his question: 'Lord, to whom shall we go? You have the words of eternal life' (John 6:68). Let us draw from the springs of salvation for ourselves and for the entire parched world" (ibid., 101).

In April 1941, the German "lightning war" machine invaded Greece and Yugoslavia. As country after country fell to the Nazi army, the Jews living in those countries fell into German hands. Already, the Nazis were killing Jews in huge numbers.

Starting September 1, 1941, Edith and her sister Rosa, now a portress for the nuns, were forced to wear on their clothing the yellow star of David, on which was inscribed the word *Jude*, German for "Jew." The Stein sisters also had to appear before Occupation Force magistrates in Maastricht and in Amsterdam, following regulations. "Notice was given that all non-Aryan German residents in Holland were stateless; they were to report by December 15 for deportation from the country," wrote the editor of Edith's memoir in her follow-up chronology of the events. "The Carmelite Nuns [in Echt] wrote to the French-speaking Carmel of Le Pâquier in Switzerland; one of the novices there knew Edith from those long-ago days when she had lectured in Switzerland. A haven was sought for Rosa with a religious congregation not far from Le Pâquier. But such correspondence was very slow-moving; and the official papers that had to be obtained in Holland, in Switzerland, and from Rome, since Edith was a professed religious, were so numerous and so reluctantly granted that the whole effort failed" (*Life*, 430).

In the summer of 1941, Edith completed an article on the "Symbolic Theology of Pseudo-Dionysius," which she wrote for a philosophical journal in the United States. During this time in Echt, Edith had been working on a new work, *The Science of the Cross*, a phenomenological study of the life, theology, and poetry of St. John of the Cross. The term "Science of the Cross" was coined by Edith, who aimed to explain the term "science" as both a theology of the Cross and a school of the Cross (see Irey, "Sister Benedicta," 9). "Sr. Benedicta wanted to show the life and spiritual evolution of John by extending his teachings on the Cross into a philosophy of the person. She addresses questions regarding the destiny and essence of the human being and expresses those laws which govern spiritual being, summing these up in her term *Science of the Cross*," wrote Sister Ruth Miriam Irey in her essay. "Sr. Benedicta begins her work by showing how

John in taking the title 'of the Cross' symbolized the ideal he sought to fulfill. This title also expressed the essential character of the Discalced Reform, 'the life of the Carmelite was to follow Christ in the way of the Cross, indeed sharing in the Cross of Christ.' In order to understand the Cross, one must have *holy objectivity* (be reborn by the Holy Spirit), which allows the soul to be formed in a free manner. *If the mystery of the Cross becomes an inner form it grows into the Science of the Cross*" (ibid.). On a personal, spiritual level, "the spirituality described in a passage here was now hers: 'Thus, the bridal union of the soul with God for which it is created is purchased through the cross, perfected with the cross, and sealed for all eternity with the cross'" (Oben, *Edith Stein*, 35).

Edith looks at each of John's works, "first describing them individually and then comparing them in order to show John's own ascent through the Dark Night and into the Mystical Union of Love," emphasized Irey. "She uses the Dark Night not only as a symbol, but also as a living reality into which the one ascending towards God is plunged. Her description of the Dark Night is thought ... to be illuminating as it not only shows how well the phenomenological method can be employed but also because it describes the state of soul and prayer of Sr. Benedicta herself" (Irey, "Sister Benedicta," 10). In *The Science of the Cross*, Edith "explains this connection between glory and suffering," wrote the Carmelite Priors General in their circular to Carmelites worldwide. "The passion and death of Christ consume our sins in fire. Therefore, as long as we accept this truth, through our faith, and try to follow Jesus, he will lead us through his passion and cross to the glory of resurrection. Edith was to combine this belief with the experience of contemplation that, passing through purification, would reach union of love with God: 'This explains its twofold character. It is death and resurrection. After the Dark Night, the Living Flame shines forth.' This is how the 'Science of the Cross' is possessed" (Maccise and Chalmers, "Losing to Win").

As Hilda Graef, translator of *The Science of the Cross* into English, noted, Edith begins her discussion on the doctrine of the Cross "with a very illuminating comparison between the Cross as a sign and the Night as a symbol." Edith's analysis of the twofold meaning of the night symbol, Graef concluded, "is one of the finest examples of the phenomenological method applied to mystical teaching" (Graef, *Scholar*, 211).

In Edith's own words, as translated and quoted by Graef:

> The night is something of nature: the opposite of the light, enveloping us and all things. It is not an object (*Gegenstand*) in the true sense of the word: it does not stand over against us, nor does it stand upon itself.... It is invisible and formless. And yet we perceive it; indeed it is much nearer to us than all objects and forms, it is much more closely related to our being. Just as the light causes the things and their visible qualities to stand out, so the night swallows them up and threatens to swallow us up, too.... At the same time our own being is not only outwardly threatened by the dangers that are hidden in the night, but it is also inwardly affected by it. The night takes away the use of our senses, it impedes our movements, paralyzes our faculties; it condemns us to solitude and makes us our own selves shadowy and ghostlike. It is a foretaste of death. And this has not only a natural, but also a psychological and spiritual significance.... The dark and uncanny night has as its contrast the gentle, magic night, flooded by the soft light of the moon. This night

does not swallow up the things but lights up their nocturnal aspect. All that is hard, sharp or crude is now softened
and smoothed; features which in the clear daylight never
appear are here revealed.... The dark night, too, has values of its own. It makes an end of the noise and bustle of
the day; it brings quiet and peace. And there is a deep and
grateful rest in the peace of the night. (ibid., 211–212).

Edith, who was responsible for the subject matter for meditation at the Echt Carmel, used excerpts from John of the Cross's
Ascent to Mount Carmel. "That was also my meditation material
for my retreat before Clothing [taking on the Carmelite habit].
Then each year I would go one step further—in the volumes of
holy Father John (of the Cross), but that does not mean I kept up
with it. I am still way down at the foot of the mount," she wrote
in a letter dated November 1940 (*Self-Portrait*, 327). Ultimately,
Edith's work, however, was left unfinished, cut short by her arrest.

On her final meditation written at Echt for the feast of the
Exaltation of the Cross—September 14, 1941—Edith again
tackles the meaning of freedom and personal choice, noting
that the created will is "called to come into unison with the
divine will." While it is "constrained by creatures that pull and
pressure it in directions straying from the development of the
nature desired by God," the human will continues to retain the
possibility of choice. Ultimately, Edith emphasizes, the way to
purity of heart lies in the following of Christ, the Son of Man,
"who not only promptly obeyed his heavenly Father, but also
subjected himself to people who imposed the Father's will on
him" (*Hidden Life*, 103).

In words that seem to anticipate the events that would tran-
spire in the following months, Edith reminds her Sisters of their

holy duty to observe the "precept of enclosure, to lead without hindrance a life hidden with Christ in God." But if "some external force were to cut us off from receiving the sacraments, [God] could compensate us, superabundantly, in some other way.... If we are faithful and are then driven out into the street, the Lord will send his angels to encamp themselves around us, and their invisible pinions will enclose our souls more securely than the highest and strongest walls. We do not need to wish for this to happen. We may ask that the experience be spared us, but only with the solemn and honestly intended addition: Not mine, but your will be done!" (ibid., 103).

To celebrate Edith's fiftieth birthday on October 12, 1941, the Sisters in the Carmel of Echt created their own skit of the patriarchs, as described in the book of Ecelesiasticus (Sirach). Edith describes the jovial event in a letter to Mother Johanna van Weersth in Beek: "I was not at all prepared for so much celebration! Just think, Your Reverence—I saw not only Abraham, but Enoch and Noah as well, Isaac and Jacob, Moses and Aaron, David, Elijah and Elisha.... Abraham was a most distinguished personage (Mother Subprioress)," Edith wrote, showing her sense of humor. "As for Moses, only his nose was impressive; the rest of him was small and quaint; the reverse of his Tablet of the Commandments was seen to be last week's kitchen list (Sister Agatha)" (*Self-Portrait*, 336). This would be Edith's last birthday.

Aware that "through my vows I am obliged to make every effort to be able to continue living according to our holy Rule," Edith wrote Dr. Hilde Vérène Borsinger of Bern, Switzerland, on New Year's Eve, 1941, asking for her assistance. "My sister Rosa and I complied [with reporting to Occupation Forces] because failing to do so would have incurred a severe penalty. But

I immediately drafted a petition for us to be permitted to remain in the Carmel of Echt and to be taken off the list of [deportees]; the petition is now being typed. But in case that fails we have to look for alternative possibilities," Edith wrote matter-of-factly of the expected deportation. "More than anything else, our Reverend Mother would like to put us up with the Carmelites of the Divine Heart (the Sisters of Sittard) in one of their Swiss convents, until such a time as a return will be possible (?). ... If we are unable to get out in this way, we will be deported by the authorities in any case" (ibid., 342).

On January 20, 1942, the Third Reich's official plan for the "Jewish problem" became the "Final Solution," the extermination of every Jew in Europe. According to the notes of the Nazi meeting that day, "'Europe is to be combed through from West to East in the course of the practical implementation of the final solution.... The evacuated Jews will be taken, group by group, to the so-called transit ghettos, in order to be transported further east from there.' Their 'Final Solution' was the planned destruction of all eleven million Jews in the countries Germany already controlled and the ones they expected to conquer."[25] On March 1, 1942, transport trains began to arrive at Auschwitz.

That April, in a letter to her friends, the Dominican Sisters of Speyer, Edith confided, "Humanly speaking, my sister Rosa and I are in a somewhat precarious situation. But as far as we know there will be no change before the end of the war. We are leaving everything confidently to Providence, and calmly go about our duties" (ibid., 346). Again, in a follow-up letter in April to her friend Dr. Hilde Borsinger of Bern, Edith shares these thoughts:

[25] David A. Adler, *We Remember the Holocaust* (New York: Scholastic, 1989), 64.

"I would also like to thank you sincerely for your kind note of January 23. Since I have had no further word from you, I take it that you have received (in Bern) the same answer we had here from the Superior General of the Carmelite Sisters of the Divine Heart: that entering Switzerland is impossible. At the end of January we had to go to Maastricht about our affairs and to Amsterdam at the end of March.... In the questionnaire we had to fill out we gave the U.S.A. as our destination. In the meantime, I have also received a letter from a Spanish Carmel urging me to come there, but that would also be impossible now.... We were assured that there could be no thought of emigrating before the end of the war. And we cannot possibly prepare today for what is going to happen then. So we continue to lead our lives calmly and leave the future to him who alone knows anything about it" (ibid., 347–348).

By July, the Carmelite monastery at Le Pâquier in the Canton Fribourg had opened its doors to Edith, and, an hour away from the Carmel, a convent of Third Order Carmelites to Rosa. "The two houses have certified, to the aliens' office of the police, that they will provide for us for our lifetimes," Edith wrote a friend and former colleague from Speyer. Still, she admitted, "The big question remains: will we be given permission here (by the Nazi occupation forces) to leave (the country).... But I will accept whatever God arranges" (ibid., 350).

On the feast of Pentecost, 1942, Edith presented the Prioress in Echt with what would be her last known poetic message before her deportation and death. Standing near the threshold of eternity, Edith remained solid in her surrender and trust in a God who is Love. The text is in the form of seven stanzas intended to be recited during the Pentecost novenas and organized as an illustrated little booklet (*Selected Writings*, 95, 99).

The Last Days

Are you not the sweet manna
Which flows from the heart of the Son
Into mine,
Food for angels and for the blessed?
He who from death to life arose,
Has awakened me, too, to new life,
From the sleep of death,
New life he gives me day by day.
Someday his abundance will completely flow
    through me,
Life of Your life — yes, You Yourself:

        Holy Spirit —
        Eternal life!

Are You the sweet song of love, and of holy awe,
Resounding ever round God's throne triune,
Which unifies the pure tone of all beings,
Within itself?
The harmony which fits the limbs to the head,
So that each blissfully finds the secret meaning
Of His being,
And exudes it with gladness freely dissolved
In Your streams:

        Holy Spirit —
        Eternal jubilation.

As soon as the Nazis occupied the Netherlands, they began mass deportation of the Jews. On July 6, 1942, Anne Frank's family went into hiding. Less than three weeks later, the Dutch bishops — led by Archbishop Johannes de Jong and including Bishop Lemmens — publicly condemned the Nazi persecution of the Jews in a pastoral letter read from the pulpit at every Mass. In the pastoral letter, signed on July 20, 1942, and read the following Sunday, the bishops informed the Dutch Catholics that they had sent a telegram to the commander of the Nazi occupation forces in Holland demanding the cessation of actions being taken against the Jewish citizens as "contrary to the deepest conviction of the Dutch people and ... to God's commands of justice and mercy." The Third Reich retaliated by arresting all non-Aryan Roman Catholics in Holland. As the July 30, 1942, journal entry of Dr. William Harster, "Commanding Officer of Security Police and the Public Security Administration in charge of The Hague," explicitly notes: "Since the Catholic bishops have interfered in something that does not concern them, deportation of all Catholic Jews will be speeded up and completed within the coming week. No appeals for clemency shall be considered. On Sunday, August 2, *Generalkommissar* Schmidt will publicly respond to the bishops' intervention at the Party gathering in Limburg" (Herbstrith, *Edith Stein*, 191).

On July 30, official correspondence lists the number of Jews registered as Catholics throughout Holland to be 722. An official memorandum the following day advises that, to date, 6,000 Jews in all had been deported from Holland without interference. The same memorandum notes that 4,000 Jews who registered as Christians had been gathered in one camp, possibly as a step toward bribing the churches to stop protesting general deportation (see *Life*, 431).

In the meantime, Edith's brother Paul Stein and his wife, Gertrude, were among 1,100 Jews from Breslau deported on July 27, 1942, to the concentration camp at Theresienstadt, the name the Germans gave the Czechoslovakian town of Terezin, near Prague. Their sister Elfriede "Frieda" Tworoger was also

deported from Riebnig, in the Protectorate (formerly Czechoslovakia), were she had been forcibly "resettled," and sent to
Theresienstadt.

Edith celebrated a feast especially meaningful to her — the
feast of St. Peter in Chains, no longer part of the Catholic liturgy — on August 1, 1941. Twelve years earlier, in a letter to
Benedictine Sister Adelgundis Jaegerschmid, Edith wrote: "St.
Peter in Chains is also a feast I particularly like, not as honoring
him, but as a commemoration of being freed from fetters through
the ministry of angels. How many chains have already been removed in this fashion, and how blessed it will be when the last
of them falls away. Until then, one must continue bearing quietly
those (chains) that are still one's portion — the more quietly we
do so, the less we feel them. And, after all, one must not meddle
in the angel's business" (*Self-Portrait*, 65).

The next day, on Sunday, August 2, 1942, at 5:00 P.M., after
Edith Stein had read the point of meditation that began silent
prayer at the Echt convent — the silence was interrupted by loud
pounding on the door. Along with her sister Rosa, Edith Stein
was seized by the Gestapo and taken away. The last words that
are remembered to have been uttered by Edith as the two sisters
left the convent were to Rosa, "Come, let us go for our people."

The exact details of Edith's final days will probably never
be fully known. Records show that Catholic prisoners of Jewish
background were transported by train to an intermediate station
in Amersfoort, followed by the assembly camp of Westerbork, the
central detention camp in the east of the Netherlands, not far
from the German border, from which all Dutch Jews — including
two years later, Anne Frank — were sent east. Westerbork would
be the last stop before Auschwitz for more than one hundred
thousand Dutch Jews.

Edith Stein: St. Teresa Benedicta of the Cross

Etty Hillesum, a twenty-seven-year-old Jewish woman from Amsterdam, recorded in letters (now published) to her friends the sights and smells of Westerbork:

> Suddenly there was a village of wooden barracks, set between heath and sky, with a glaringly yellow lupin field in the middle and barbed wire all around. And there were human lives as well, thick as flies.... There is mud, so much mud that somewhere between your ribs you need to have a great deal of inner sunshine if you don't want to become the psychological victim of it all. The physical effects, such as broken shoes and wet feet, you will certainly understand. Although the camp buildings are all one story, you can hear as many accents as if the Tower of Babel had been erected in our midst: Bavaria and Groningen, Saxony and Limburg. The Hague and East Friesland; you can hear German with a Polish accent and German with a Russian accent; you find all sorts of dialects from Holland and Berlin—all in an area of half a kilometer square.... On the one hand it is a stable community in the making, a forced one to be sure.... And on the other hand, it is a camp for a people in transit, great waves of human beings constantly washed in from the cities and provinces ... of the Netherlands—only to be deported a few days later to meet their unknown destiny.[26]

Eyewitness reports of Edith at Westerbork by survivors and other witnesses show a woman of remarkable interior strength,

---

[26] Etty Hillesum, *An Interrupted Life: The Diaries, 1941–1943 and Letters from Westerbork* (New York: Henry Holt, 1996), 242, 245–246.

much as she had been at so many other difficult times in her life. Early biographers have recorded statements by survivors, witnesses, and even one by a Dutch guard of Westerbork. A report by Frau Bromberg, the mother of a Dominican priest, describes Edith Stein's attitude to the perverse situation:

> What distinguished Edith Stein from the rest of the sisters was her silence. Rather than seeming fearful, to me she appeared oppressed. Maybe the best way I can explain it is to say that she carried so much pain that it hurt to see her smile. She hardly ever spoke; but often she would look at her sister Rosa with a sorrow beyond words. As I write, it occurs to me that she probably understood what was awaiting them. She was, after all, the only one who had escaped from Germany as a refugee, and this would have given her a much better idea.... As I say, in my opinion, she was thinking about the suffering that lay ahead. Not her own suffering—she was too resigned for that—but the suffering that was in store for the others. Every time I think of her in the barracks, the same picture comes to mind: a Pietà without the Christ. (Herbstrith, *Edith Stein*, 182–183)

Another eyewitness, survivor Julius Marcan of Cologne, testified:

> It was Edith Stein's complete calm and self-possession that marked her out from the rest of the prisoners. There was a spirit of indescribable misery in the camp; the new prisoners, especially, suffered from extreme anxiety. Edith Stein went among the women like an angel, comforting, helping, and consoling them. Many of the mothers were

on the brink of insanity and had sat moaning for days, without giving any thought to their children. Edith Stein immediately set about taking care of these little ones. She washed them, combed their hair, and tried to make sure they were fed and cared for. (ibid., 183)

But official records are scarce.

There is the form letter in which the Swiss consulate turned down Edith and Rosa's application to enter that country as refugees. The letter, dated August 3, 1942, simply states, "Immigration is not desirable at this time." By that time, however, the two sisters were already in the hands of the Gestapo.

From Drente-Westerbork, Barracks 36, there are several notes written by Edith and sent to the Echt community. In a letter dated August 4, she described, "During the past night we left the transit-station (Amersfoort) and landed here early this morning.... All the Catholics are together and in our dormitory we have all the nuns.... We have asked many people to relay news to you....We are very calm and cheerful. Of course, so far there has been no Mass and Communion; maybe that will come later. Now we have a chance to experience a little how to live purely from within." Edith also requested that the Sisters send them their ID cards and ration cards, explaining, "So far we have lived entirely on the generosity of the others" (*Self-Portrait*, 350–351).

A note attached from Rosa declared, "In this brief time we have experienced a great deal; one lives together with the others and everywhere people help each other," with a final line, "we [are not upset] at all." Edith also enclosed in the letter a message on a separate piece of paper addressed to the Swiss consulate: "Enable us as soon as possible to cross the border. Our monastery will take care of travel expenses" (ibid., 351).

The Last Days

The next day, August 5, Edith's letter to Echt indicated, "A [Red Cross] nurse from [Amsterdam] intends to speak today with the Consul. Here, every petition (on behalf) of fully Jewish Catholics has been forbidden since yesterday.... According to plans, a transport will leave on Friday.... We count on your prayers. There are so many persons here who need some consolation and they expect it from the Sisters" (ibid., 352).

And on the final note to Mother Superior, dated "[Thursday,] August 6, 1942," and written on two small pages from an appointment calendar, Edith wrote (ibid., 353):

> Dear Mother,
> A Mother Superior from one of the convents arrived last evening with suitcases for her child and now offers to take some short letters along. Early tomorrow a transport leaves (Silesia or Czechoslovakia??).
> What is most necessary: woolen stockings, two blankets. For Rosa all the warm underwear and whatever was in the laundry; for us both towels and wash cloths. Rosa also has no toothbrush, no Cross and no rosary. I would like the next volume of the breviary (so far I have been able to pray gloriously). Our identity cards, registration cards [as Jews], and ration cards.
> A thousand thanks, greetings to all, Y[our] R[everence]'s grateful child,
> B[enedicta]

On the fortieth anniversary of Edith's death, a story in the Cologne newspaper told the account of a postal employee named Johannes Wieners, who was sent in 1942 to the eastern war zone where the Sixth German Army was fighting the Russians. According to the editor of Edith's *Life in a Jewish Family*:

Edith Stein: St. Teresa Benedicta of the Cross

On the 7th of August, 1942, [Wieners] and the others in his unit were standing in the switching area of the railroad depot in Breslau since their engine had been uncoupled for servicing. A freight train pulled into the station on the track next to theirs. A minute or so later, a guard opened a sliding door on one of the cars. With dismay, Wieners noticed it was packed with people who were jammed together, cowering on the floor. The stench coming from the car almost overpowered the men standing outside. Then a woman in nun's clothing stepped into the opening. Wieners looked at her with such commiseration that she spoke to him: "It's awful. We have nothing by way of containers for sanitation needs."

Looking into the distance and then across the town, she said, "This is my beloved hometown. I will never see it again." When he looked at her, questioningly, she added, very hesitantly: "We are riding to our death." He was profoundly shocked and asked, in all seriousness: "Do your companion prisoners believe that also?" Her answer came even more hesitantly. "It's better that they do not know it." ... Johannes Wieners served for a time and then was taken a prisoner of war. When, much later, he was back in Germany, he saw a picture of Edith Stein, accompanying an article about her. He was sure she was the nun he had seen on August 7, 1942. (*Life*, 434–435)

But much of the official trail of the Stein sisters is lost here. Approximately seven hundred Dutch Catholics of Jewish background, including some three hundred nuns and priests, were arrested along with Rosa and Edith. In 1950, when the official Dutch *Gazette* published the names of all Jews who had been deported from Holland on August 7, 1942, the following entry was found:

> Number 44074: Edith Theresia Hedwig Stein, Echt
> Born—October 12, 1891, Breslau
> Died—August 9, 1942

The ninth was assigned as the date of record because of judicial testimony that there were no survivors from the transport (see Herbstrith, *Edith Stein*, 190). There are no formal records of the Stein sisters at Auschwitz because the prisoners designated for death right from the train were never registered by camp records.

One can imagine, however, how it all came to pass.

Men, women, and children were herded like cattle into freight trains at Westerbork. Yelling. Crying. Screaming. Whimpering. People pushed, one on top of the other, without food or water, until the doors opened days later at Auschwitz-Birkenau—one of six death camps for Jews and other enemies of the German nation. The ones who died on the trains were later carried out by prisoners and thrown onto a wagon to be burned, like yard waste. Surely, Edith and Rosa would have stood together at the *Rampe*, the railway platform within the camp where selections were held after unloading from the trains. Huge chimneys, smoke, and a terrible smell were unmistakable. Auschwitz SS officials, most notably Josef Mengele, would quickly determine whether a prisoner was able to work. First the men were separated from the women. Then those who were chosen as capable of working as slave laborers—the young and strong—were sent to one side. The ones chosen to work, lived. In Auschwitz, a number tattooed on the arm meant life.

Edith and Rosa and all the others who were not selected for work—children, mothers with young children, the elderly, invalids—were told they needed to be cleaned of lice. "They were led to a waiting area made to look like the hall of a bathhouse. Attendants, often dressed in white, distributed towels and pieces of soap. The prisoners were told to undress and to fold their clothes neatly. And they were told to remember where they left their clothes so that after their showers they could reclaim them" (Adler, *We Remember*, 78–79). The two sisters would have certainly stood together, held each other, found ways to comfort each other—as everyone stood like silhouettes holding on to the last shreds of their humanity.

And no doubt they prayed for strength—perhaps out loud to comfort the other women—to the God to whom Edith had already totally surrendered. As the women were crowded into these "bathhouses," perhaps Edith, aware of the perverse reality, recited out loud a prayer that would have been common knowledge to the terrified women around her—the Sh'ma: "Hear, O Israel: the Lord our God, the Lord is one," a line of prayer said as a statement of faith when death is approaching. Possibly, Edith would have continued by reciting the Our Father, noting the words "forgive us our trespasses as we forgive those who trespass against us," finally adding the Hail Mary, "... Holy Mary, Mother of God, pray for us sinners now and at the hour of our death."

"There were shower heads and fake drains in the bathhouses, but no water. The 'attendants' often shot bullets into the room to force the prisoners to crowd closer together. The doors were locked. SS guards wearing gas masks dropped poison pellets through an opening in the ceiling. Poison fumes filled the room. At times Nazi guards watched through peepholes as [the innocent women] gasped and struggled for air in the last moments of life. When the screaming stopped, the Nazis knew the Jews were dead. The gassings took from three to fifteen minutes. The doors were opened. The bodies dragged out with metal hooks. Wedding rings were pulled off. Mouths were pried open in search of gold-filled teeth.... The dead women's hair was used to fill pillows and mattresses" (ibid., 79). The bodies were then taken to one of Auschwitz's five crematoria, ovens, were they were burned. "Some of the ashes from these ovens were used to fertilize German gardens. The skin of some dead Jews was used to make lampshades. The fat was used to make soap. Hair was used to make a coarse cloth used in industry" (ibid., 80).

According to the information available, it is almost certain that Edith and her sister Rosa died on August 9, 1942—two of the 1.1 million people estimated to have died in the gas chambers in Auschwitz, Poland, only 150 miles from Edith's native and beloved Breslau. Her sister, Frieda (née Stein) Tworoger died sometime that year at the Theresienstadt "model camp." Paul Stein died on April 29, 1943, his wife on March 18—both at Theresienstadt (see *Aunt Edith*, 152, 156). Twenty-seven-year-old Eva Stein, the daughter of Edith's brother Arno, was deported from Breslau, perhaps sometime in 1942. In addition to being Jewish, as a retarded person Eva was seen by the Nazis as one of the "unworthy." When Eva could not pass the mental exams at the consulate, her family migrated to the United States by 1938 without her. She, too, is assumed to have died at Theresienstadt (see ibid., 166–167).

Responding to the Carmelites' search for traces of official records on Sister Benedicta of the Cross, the Bureau of Information of the Netherlands Red Cross reported in 1958 that, according to the papers kept in their archives, an Edith Teresa Hedwig Stein who had been arrested in Echt on August 2, 1942, was taken to Amersfoort (Holland) and on August 5 handed over in Westerbork. She was in the transport that left Westerbork on August 7, 1942, and arrived at Auschwitz in the early hours of the ninth. "The above named person is to be considered as having died on 9 August, 1942, in Auschwitz" (*Life*, 432).

Part 5

The Legacy of Edith Stein

Edith Stein's family in 1895. Back row, starting from left: Arno, Else, Siegfried (Edith's father), Elfriede, and Paul. Front row, same order: Rosa, Auguste (Edith's mother), Edith, and Erna. The photograph of Edith's father, who died in 1893, is superimposed.

Edith (right) and her sister Erna, circa 1900.

Edith as a student in Göttingen, circa 1913–1914.

Edith (foreground) and her sister Erna (right) on a hike with friends during summer vacation in 1911.

Edith, in 1921, with her cousin's son.

Edith (left) in 1926 with students during her years as an instructor at St. Magdalena's Convent in Speyer.

Edith during her years at Speyer, 1923–1931.

Edith on her Clothing Day, April 15, 1934, in the Köln Carmel, when she took the religious name Teresa Benedicta of the Cross, O.C.D.

Passport photo taken for Edith's transfer to the Echt, Holland, Carmel in 1938, following the violence of the *Kristallnacht*.

Edith and her sister Rosa in the garden of the
Carmel in Echt, Holland, circa 1939.

Chapter 16

Peace That Surpasses Understanding

The life and death of Etty Hillesum in many ways parallels that of Edith Stein. Born in 1914 in Middelburg, Netherlands, Hillesum was a young intellectual Jewish woman who left behind diaries and a collection of letters — all composed in the shadow of the *Shoah*, a word that literally means "catastrophe." Like Edith's, Hillesum's life story was a personal, steadfast crusade toward truth. At the time of her death in Auschwitz, Hillesum was a young, educated, courageous woman with professional ambitions. Although her impassioned life was at times tormented and void of God, it was in the midst of her physical and emotional suffering that Hillesum found the meaning of life that she had been so ardently searching for.

"I don't feel in anybody's clutches," she wrote in her journal in July of 1942. "I feel safe in God's arms ... and no matter whether I am sitting at this beloved old desk now, or in a bare room in the Jewish district, or perhaps in a labor camp under SS guards in a month's time — I shall always feel safe in God's arms. They may well succeed in breaking me physically, but no more than that. I may face cruelty and deprivation the likes of which I cannot imagine in even my wildest fantasies. Yet all this is as nothing to the immeasurable expanse of my faith in God and my inner receptiveness" (Hillesum, *Interrupted Life*, 176).

Although Etty Hillesum lacked the knowledge of formal faith that Edith had been graced with, her experience at the hands of the Nazis nevertheless led her to the hands of God. As she grew spiritually, Hillesum also became painfully aware of the gruesome reality faced by the Jews—and she faced it with courage and faith. "I must admit a new insight into my life and find a place for it," she wrote in 1942. With words that echoed Edith's predictions of the Nazi agenda for the Jews, Hillesum added, "What is at stake is our impending destruction and annihilation, we can have no more illusions about that. They are out to destroy us completely, we must accept that and go on from there," she summarized. "Today I was filled with terrible despair, and I shall have to come to terms with that as well.... I shall not be bitter if others fail to grasp what is happening to us Jews. I work and continue to live with the same conviction, and I find life meaningful—yes, meaningful.... Living and dying, sorrow and joy, the blisters on my feet and the jasmine behind the house, the persecution, the unspeakable horrors—it is all as one in me, and I accept it all as one mighty whole and begin to grasp it better.... And that is why I must try to live a good and faithful life to my last breath: so that those who come after me do not have to start all over again.... Yes, we carry everything within us, God and Heaven and Hell and Earth and Life and Death and all of history. The externals are simply so many props; everything we need is within us ... and we must begin with ourselves, every day anew" (ibid., 153–155).

Etty Hillesum was one of the "residents" of Westerbork the day Edith and Rosa Stein—along with sixty-one other Catholics of Jewish heritage, many of them cloistered religious—were brought to the overcrowded Nazi transit camp. Etty wrote describing them in a letter and her diary: "There was a remarkable day when the Jewish Catholics or Catholic Jews—whichever you want to call them—arrived, nuns and priests wearing the yellow star on their habits. I remember two young novices, twins, with identical beautiful, dark ghetto faces and serene, childish eyes peering out from under their skullcaps. They said with mild surprise they had been fetched at half past four from morning mass, and that they had eaten red cabbage in Amersfoort" (ibid., 248).

Etty Hillesum eventually boarded the dreaded transport from Westerbork to "the east," a year after Edith—on September 7, 1943. And, like Edith, Etty did not delude herself about the situation she was facing. Although no one at Westerbork had heard of the gas chambers, Etty knew she would not survive. "Very well then," she wrote, "this new certainty, that what they are after is our total destruction, I accept it. I know it now, and I shall not burden others with my fears" (ibid., 155).

And yet—like the stories related by eyewitnesses about Edith—Etty Hillesum stepped onto the Westerbork platform and train transport a woman at peace with herself and her reality. In a letter to common friends in Amsterdam, one of Etty's friends described Etty's departure from the Westerbork transit camp: "Talking gaily, smiling, a kind word for everyone she met on the way, full of sparkling humor, perhaps just a touch of sadness, but every inch the Etty you all know so well.... I saw Mother, Father H., and Mischa [Hillesum's parents and brother] board car No. 1. Etty finished up in No. 12, having first stopped to look for a friend in car No. 14, who was pulled out again at the last minute. Then a shrill whistle and the 1,000 'transport cases' were moving out. Another flourish from Mischa, who waved through a crack in No. 1, a cheerful 'Bye' from Etty in No. 12, and they were gone." Before they left the Netherlands, "Etty threw a postcard addressed to (a friend) out of the train. It was found and sent by farmers: 'We left the camp singing,' it read. They reached Auschwitz on 10 September 1943. That very day, her mother and father were gassed. On 30 November 1943, the Red Cross reported the death of Etty Hillesum" (ibid., xxii).

To those of us born after these incomprehensible and appalling events took place, to the majority of us who have not and will never experience such dehumanizing and evil acts at the hands of others—the image of a woman boarding a train smiling, in spite of knowing it was synonymous with her death—is absolutely inconceivable. Etty Hillesum and Edith Stein were not oblivious of their future. They recognized the evil around them. They named it. They still chose to face it with joy and courage. The fact that both Etty Hillesum and Edith wrote notes on those last days that appear to us, later observers, as too mundane or filled with hope to reflect the life choices of a martyr, only shows our personal ignorance as "readers" of the events. They were not pretending, or as some critics have said of Edith, obviously unaware of their fate. Etty and Edith emerged fearless and confident—even while embracing the suffering—because their lives were no longer determined by external forces.

As Etty wrote in her journal, "My acceptance is not indifference or helplessness. I feel deep moral indignation at a regime that treats human beings in such a way. . . . It is not as if I want to fall into the arms of destruction with a resigned smile—far from it. I am only bowing to the inevitable, and even as I do so I am sustained by the certain knowledge that ultimately they cannot rob us of anything that matters" (ibid., 176–177). Ultimately, the German Nazis controlled the women's external freedom, but they could not take away their inner peace. As Edith once wrote, "I have an ever deeper and firmer belief that nothing is merely an accident when seen in the light of God, that my whole life down to its smallest details have been marked out for me in the plan of divine Providence and has a completely coherent meaning in God's all seeing eye" (Oben, *Edith Stein*, 77). Edith had attained what all of us hope for—the peace that surpasses all understanding.

Chapter 17

⌒

Jewish by Birth, Martyr by Death

The word "martyr," whose root is the Greek *martyr* or *martys*, literally means "to witness." A martyr is a person who voluntarily chooses to die or be killed as the penalty for witnessing or giving testimony to a religious belief. The word "martyr" was first used in reference to early Christians who were put to death for their confession of faith. The essence of being a martyr is closely aligned to remembering. These early Christian martyrs were witnesses not to what they had seen with their eyes, but to what they knew in their hearts. They believed, they remembered, and they witnessed with their life—and through their death. We, the community of faith, remember them in thanksgiving for their witness of faith.

In front of an urn filled with ashes of the victims, an eternal light is kept burning at the Yad Vashem Memorial to Holocaust victims in Jerusalem, a center for study of the *Shoah*. A sign nearby proclaims: "The mystery of redemption lies in remembrance." To remember is to honor a life, to honor a belief, to honor a faith. As Catholic Christians we remember those who witnessed with their life because their life story leads us to the Truth they chose to die for. For Christians, to die as martyrs is, therefore, a privilege, an honor. But while remembering is at the essence of the *Shoah*, those of the Jewish faith differ sharply with the Christian's view of martyrdom. As Edith's niece Susanne Batzdorff, an observant Jew, plainly notes, martyrdom is simply not extolled as an ideal in the Jewish faith and tradition (see *Selected Writings*, 118).

Although she was outspoken about her Christian beliefs, Edith never denied her Jewish origins. In fact, all the way to her death, she refused to see the Jews as disadvantaged before God.

As a cloistered Carmelite, Edith not only saw herself as still a member of the Stein family, but she was also present to her family — and all the people of Israel — in her heart and mind, in the unique and privileged grace that only someone living a total life of prayer can offer. "Edith made her own the suffering of the Jewish people," Pope John Paul II wrote in his apostolic letter naming Edith a co-patron of Europe. "At the time, she felt that in the systematic extermination of the Jews the Cross of Christ was being laid on her people, and she herself took part in it by her deportation and execution in the infamous camp of Auschwitz-Birkenau. Her voice merged with the cry of all the victims of that appalling tragedy, but at the same time was joined to the cry of Christ on the Cross which gives to human suffering a mysterious and enduring fruitfulness."

There is no question that the six million victims of the *Shoah* deserve much more than our sympathy. They require, to use Edith's word, our empathy. And they deservingly insist that we remember — because the mystery of redemption lies, indeed, in remembrance. Those of us who are Catholic Christians must, as the Pope emphasized at Edith Stein's canonization in 1998, remember the *Shoah*, "that cruel plan to exterminate a people, a plan to which millions of our Jewish brothers and sisters fell victim.... I raise an anguished cry: May such criminal deeds never be repeated against any ethnic group, against any race, in any other corner of this world! It is a cry to everyone: to all people of goodwill; to all who believe in the Just and Eternal God; to all who know they are joined to Christ, the Word of God made man."

Where does that leave Edith Stein?

A *Time* magazine article published the week of Edith Stein's beatification argued that Edith's quest for a transfer to a Swiss convent — and even her request for clothing written from the barracks at Westerbork — all "indicate ignorance of her fate," her death being totally "involuntary." Other critics have argued that Edith's death at Auschwitz denied her a choice. She was put to death by the Nazis for her Jewish birth, her genealogy. And, as *The New Yorker* argued in an article published eight months after her canonization, "Now, by elevating her death not only above her own life but above the deaths of six million Jews, the Church has made Edith Stein a flash point instead of a bridge."

Yet even a writer like Patricia Hampl, who in her essay on Stein, "A Book Sealed with Seven Seals," clearly states that she does not think that Edith Stein should have been canonized, finds Edith's conversion authentic and compelling. The paradox of Edith Stein's life, explains Hampl, "was not a contradiction to be debated but a truth to be lived" (*Stories*, 108). Edith Stein "bore a crushing burden of paradox with simplicity, certainty, and humility. She went where she had to go — into the Catholic communion when commanded by faith; then, even deeper, into the cloister of Carmel, and finally, crammed into a fetid boxcar, to Auschwitz" (ibid.).

While the Pope's proclamation that Edith Stein died at Auschwitz as a martyr created a lot of controversy and critical debate among the secular and religious press, what is most remarkable about Edith Stein is not just how she died, but how she lived.

To understand martyrdom, in the end, is to view someone's life through the eyes of faith. Some people who view the victims of the *Shoah* can see only people without a choice. Others can view the life of a woman, like Etty Hillesum, and rather than acknowledging a heroic young woman who chose to remain and help her Jewish people, doing what she could at Westerbork, claim that she simply gave up on life. Indeed, critics will look at the life of Edith Stein and see only the surface facts. She was born Jewish. She was murdered at Auschwitz by the Nazis. She did not have a choice.

To understand martyrdom *requires* that we view a life through the eyes of faith. From the moment of her conversion—and every single act leading to that moment—Edith Stein made choices that shaped her life and reflected her faith. From the beginning, Edith made everyday choices that as a Christian she believed reflected her faith. They were often simple acts—to write a letter of encouragement, to take time to listen one-on-one to a student, to agree to give a lecture when what she wanted was simply to sit in a corner of the church and pray. And she made enormous, life-changing choices that ultimately shaped her life and led to her death. She chose to be baptized in spite of the immense personal sacrifice to her relationship with her family, especially her mother. In obedience to her spiritual advisers and for the sake of her mother, she chose to wait eleven years before entering Carmel. And even when she was forced to give up teaching in 1933 because of her Jewish blood, Edith seriously weighed all her professional options before making a decision—moving to South America to teach; relocating to a different community in Germany where her Catholic friends would support her; leaving the country. But "by that time," she wrote later, "a very different path had been revealed to me" (*Selected Writings*, 18).

Edith chose to enter Carmel rather than to find safe haven, in spite of the fact that she acknowledged the growing power of evil in her world. While a worldly critic may interpret that choice, along with Etty Hillesum's choice, as that of a woman who gave up on life—or even of someone running away from "real" life —those with the eyes of faith will recognize Edith's heart yearning to be one with God, who is Love. Over and over, Edith's choices reflect the love that guided her actions and her heart. Years later, when she was offered safety away from her sister, Edith chose to remain with Rosa to give her strength, solidarity, and encouragement. As Edith's niece reflects on that choice, she points to a passage in Jewish liturgy concerning the slaughter of the martyrs that says: "'Beloved and true were they in life, and even in death they were not divided.' That is how I picture Rosa and Edith. Alone, Edith could have found asylum in Switzerland, but she refused to accept refuge without Rosa, and in the end they met death together" (*Aunt Edith*, 163). Edith Stein chose to believe there are no coincidences, only the hand of God at work in the world.

Ultimately, to understand martyrdom is to choose to remember a life of faith with the eyes of God. Every single choice we make in life will either reflect and lead to the Truth we profess—or will lead away from it. As Edith wrote on the feast of Epiphany, January 6, 1941, "We do not know whether we shall experience the end of this year. But if we drink from the fount of the Savior each day, then each day will lead us deeper into eternal life and prepare us to throw off the burdens of this life easily and cheerfully at some time when the call of the Lord sounds. The Divine Child offers us his hand to renew our bridal bond. Let us hurry to clasp his hand. The Lord is my light and my salvation—of whom shall I be afraid?" (*Hidden Life*, 115).

Edith chose, consistently and faithfully, to clasp His hand and follow the Truth that had opened her eyes and touched her heart on the eve of her thirtieth birthday. In her own words, "When life on earth ends and everything transitory falls away, every soul will see itself 'as it is perceived'—as it appears before God. It will see to what purpose God has created it in particular and what it has become in the order of nature and mercy and, most importantly, what it has become through its own voluntary decisions" (*Daybook*, 111). As a vowed religious and a daughter of Carmel, Edith believed that her call took her a step further. "The love of Christ impels [virginal souls] to descend into the darkest night," she wrote the year before she was killed. "And no earthly maternal joy resembles the bliss of a soul permitted to enkindle the light of grace in the night of sins. The way to this is the cross" (*Hidden Life*, 104).

As Carmelite Sister Ruth Miriam Irey points out in her essay on Stein, as a philosopher, Edith sought to find what was real. "For Sr. Benedicta, reality ultimately led her to the Church, Carmel, and the Cross. The gift of natural intelligence which Edith possessed, and the thirst for knowledge which was her passion, was transformed through grace and she was lifted to the height of mystical contemplation by the Source of Knowledge. The vehicle of this transformation was the Cross. It gave her life, and it also gave her the courage to face her death and offer it up as an atoning victim for peace" ("Sister Benedicta," 19).

Unlike many people around her, Edith was extremely aware of the dangerous and destructive developments in her world and, specifically, of their consequence on the people of Israel. Early in 1933, the year the Third Reich was established, Edith was an instructor at the German Institute for Scientific Pedagogy in Münster. She recalled years later a conversation she had with a middle-class Catholic teacher who related to her "unconfirmed reports" described in American newspapers of cruelties to which Jews had been subjected. The teacher was unaware of Edith's own Jewish background. "True, I had heard of rigorous measures against the Jews before," Edith wrote. "But now a light dawned in my brain that once again God had put a heavy hand upon His people and that the fate of this people would also be mine" (*Selected Writings*, 16). As a Carmelite novice a couple of years later, Edith yearned for the day "when I shall be allowed to feel more of my vocation to the cross than I do now, since the Lord treats me once more as if I were a little child" (*Self-Portrait*, 197).

The year 1933 was designated by the Church as a Holy Year to commemorate the nineteen hundredth anniversary of the death of Jesus Christ. During Mass on the First Friday of April that year, Edith discusses further her awareness that she was to carry the Cross for her Jewish people. "I talked with the Savior and told Him that I knew that it was His cross that was now being placed upon the Jewish people; that most of them did not understand this, but that those who did, would have to take it up willingly in the name of all. I would do that. He should only show me how. At the end of the service, I was certain that I had been heard. But what this carrying of the cross was to consist in, that I did not yet know" (*Selected Writings*, 17).

For weeks during the spring of 1933, Edith also considered how she personally "could do something about the plight of the Jews." She decided to travel to Rome and request a private audience with the Holy Father and ask him for an encyclical on the subject. "Although it suited my nature to make such an overt move, I sensed that this was not yet 'of the essence.' But I did not yet know what this 'essence' really was," she wrote. Edith nevertheless made inquiries in Rome and was told that because of the tremendous crowds she would have no chance at a private audience. "I abandoned my travel plans and instead presented my request in writing. I know that my letter was delivered to the Holy Father [Pope Pius XI] unopened; sometime thereafter I received his blessing for myself and for my relatives. Nothing else happened. Later on I often wondered whether this letter might have come to his mind once in a while. For in the years that followed, that which I had predicted for the future of the Catholics in Germany came true step by step" (*Selected Writings*, 17).

As Jesuit Jan H. Nota recalled, prior to 1933, Edith Stein was indeed one of the few who recognized the catastrophe threatening the Jewish people. "Unfortunately her 1933 request to Pope Pius XI for an encyclical in defense of the Jews was not complied with at the time — due in large part to faulty handling of the matter. Nonetheless, it is heartening to know that shortly thereafter the Pope commissioned two Jesuits, Fathers La Farge and [Gundlach], to compose a document condemning racial persecution. Though the outbreak of World War II and the death of the Pope prevented the publication of their efforts, parts of their work later appeared in speeches of Pius XII" (Herbstrith, *Edith Stein*, 11).

Father Nota, who befriended Edith during those dark years she lived in Echt, recounted that Edith was aware of the growing presence of evil. "Edith Stein's wish to offer her life for world peace and the preservation of her people should not ... be taken as a manifestation of something unhealthy. Sacrifice for its own sake did not interest her; the active yearning for suffering and the retreat into subhuman passivity were both equally foreign," emphasized Father Nota, who saw Edith less than a month before her arrest and deportation. "Years earlier she had compared the study of philosophy to a walk along the edge of an abyss. Now in Carmel, once again 'on the brink,' she had discovered in Christ the meaning of human existence and suffering. What she found drew her to surrender herself to God in union with him. Edith Stein was one of those Christians who lived out of a hope transcending optimism and pessimism. At one and the same time she could enthusiastically consider the idea of emigrating to the Carmel in Bethlehem and peacefully accept the likelihood of the project's failure" (ibid., 12). As Edith Stein herself wrote, "'He who wants to keep his soul will lose it.' Thus the soul can only find itself when it is not concerned with the self.... One who belongs to Christ must experience the whole life of Christ and must some day enter upon the way of the cross, to Gethsemane and Golgotha" (*Daybook*, 87, 78).

Chapter 18

⁀

Jewish and Catholic Dilemmas

While the Catholic Church considers the recognition of saint-hood to be the highest honor it can bestow on one of her members, to the Jewish community the sainthood of Edith Stein is a challenging and disturbing matter. Theologically speaking, Edith Stein was the most significant Jewish convert to Christianity of the twentieth century, argues Professor of Jewish Studies David Novak. "In general, Jewish tradition regards such persons as apostates who have removed themselves from the normative Jewish community in a radical way, even if they still consider themselves part of the body of the Jewish people, as Stein did," Novak wrote in an article published in *First Things*. "Judaism in fact also regards such persons as part of the body of the Jewish people. 'A Jew who has sinned is still a Jew' is an important Talmudic principle. Nevertheless, an apostate is an apostate, even when a person of extraordinary intellectual and moral virtues. Our reactions in such cases, however great or small the person before us is, range from anger to sorrow. We cannot very well be indifferent."[27]

---

[27] David Novak, "Edith Stein, Apostate Saint," *First Things* (October 1999): 15.

Edith Stein: St. Teresa Benedicta of the Cross

Other Jewish critics, on the other hand, stress that while a nonpracticing, even nonbelieving, Jew is considered to be Jewish, one who embraces another faith is understood by Jewish teaching as renouncing Jewish faith and must, as a consequence, be considered no longer a Jew. According to Susanne Batzdorff, after her Aunt Edith became a Catholic, "she always remained a beloved member of the family," but "in the eyes of her Jewish family and the Jewish community from which she descended, with her conversion she ceased to be a Jew."

Nevertheless, Novak noted, "Jews have been able to dismiss most modern Jewish converts to Christianity as people motivated by social or professional ambition, self-hatred, ignorance, or mental imbalance. But anyone who knew Edith Stein or who knows anything about her life would have to admit that none of these categories applies to her. Indeed, Edith Stein comes across as *sui generis* [one of a kind]. She might be the most uniquely problematic Jew for us since Saul of Tarsus."

In addition to the question of Jewish identity, the Jewish dilemma regarding the canonization of Edith Stein centers on the understanding that *all* the victims of the *Shoah* were martyrs. And to some, singling Edith Stein out of the six million Jewish victims to Nazi genocide may be perceived as belittling rather than honoring those who died. While Catholics may look at Edith Stein as a symbol of the *Shoah*, for the Stein family, she is not the only symbol. Edith's niece Eva, her brother Paul, and her sisters Frieda and Rosa were also victims of National Socialism — Rosa on the same day as Edith.

On the other hand, Edith Stein presents an entirely different dilemma for Catholics: how to understand that Edith Stein died both as a "daughter of Israel" and as a Christian martyr. In January of 1987, the year she was beatified, the Congregation for the Causes of Saints declared Edith the first person in its four-hundred-year history to be confirmed as both confessor and martyr (see Irey, "Sister Benedicta," 19). The Church considers Edith Stein a martyr because she was killed not only for her Jewish heritage, but also for living her Catholic Faith. As Cardinal William Keeler remarked in an advisory to the Catholic bishops on the canonization of Edith Stein, "As a Church, we cannot pretend that she died as anything other than one of the six million Jews murdered in the *Shoah*. We need the reminder of Christian sinfulness that the first affirmation brings with it, as well as the spiritual challenge of the second affirmation. But we need also to remember, sensitively and compassionately, that the Jewish people do not see it that way. Nor, of course, do they need the reminder of the *Shoah* in the same way we do."[28] It was because she was Jewish, the Pope declared at Stein's canonization, that "Edith Stein was taken with her sister Rosa and many other Catholic Jews from the Netherlands to the concentration camp in Auschwitz, where she died with them in the gas chambers. Today we remember them all with deep respect. A few days before her deportation, the woman religious had dismissed the question about a possible rescue: 'Do not do it! Why should I be spared? Is it not right that I should gain no advantage from my Baptism? If I cannot share the lot of my brothers and sisters, my life, in a certain sense, is destroyed.' From now on," the Pope emphasized, "we must all stand together: human dignity is at stake. There is only one human family. The new saint also insisted on

[28] Cardinal William Keeler, "Advisory on the Implications for Catholic-Jewish Relations of the Canonization of Edith Stein," September 1998, posted on the website of the Carmelite Nuns of Baltimore, http://www.baltimorecarmel.org/saints/Stein/keeler%20advisory%20implications.htm.

this: 'Our love of neighbor is the measure of our love of God. For Christians and not only for them no one is a "stranger." The love of Christ knows no borders.'"

Edith Stein died because she was born Jewish and because she had professed the Catholic Faith. In retaliation for the Dutch bishops' pastoral letter criticizing Nazi persecution of Jews, the Germans had ordered the arrest of all priests and religious who were even one-eighth Jewish. It was under this order that Edith was arrested by the Gestapo.

Pope John Paul II noted at Edith Stein's beatification ceremony in Cologne, Germany, on May 1, 1987, that "Edith Stein died at the Auschwitz extermination camp, the daughter of a martyred people. Despite the fact that she moved from Cologne to the Dutch Carmelite community in Echt, her protection against the growing persecution of the Jews was only temporary. The Nazi policy of exterminating the Jews was rapidly implemented in Holland, too, after the country had been occupied. Jews who had converted to Christianity were initially left alone. However, when the Catholic bishops in the Netherlands issued a pastoral letter in which they sharply protested against the deportation of the Jews, the Nazi rulers reacted by ordering the extermination of the Catholic Jews as well. This was the cause of the martyrdom suffered by Sister Teresa Benedicta of the Cross together with her sister Rosa, who had also sought refuge with the Carmelites in Echt." Reflecting on Edith's accomplishments, the Pope said in 1995 that Edith Stein's conversion was reached after a painful personal search and "did not signify the refusal of her cultural and religious roots." Christ was helping her to "read the history of her people in a deeper way."

As Dr. Eugene J. Fisher, associate director for the Secretariat for Ecumenical and Interreligious Affairs for the U.S. Catholic

Bishops, noted in the introduction to *Aunt Edith*, "It is true, ironically, that she might have survived had not the bishops of Holland defied the Nazis and publicly condemned the deportations of Jews. The Nazis retaliated by swiftly rounding up and deporting all of the Jews they could identify who had converted to Catholicism (leaving alone, for the time, Jews who had converted to Protestantism since the Protestant leadership had heeded the Nazi warning to them not to go public with their equally deeply felt concerns for the Jews of Holland).... But the context, however ambiguous, of Edith Stein being killed for the sake of the witness to her adopted faith, is to the Church more than sufficient to consider her an authentic Catholic martyr even while acknowledging the primacy of the utter Jewishness of her death as merely one Jew equally among six million others" (*Aunt Edith*, 13).

From the beginning, statements on Edith Stein by the Pope and by bishops' conferences both in Europe and the United States have condemned the idea that the raising up of a convert of Jewish background for Catholic veneration may occasion movements within the Church to proselytize and convert other Jews. In the United States, the advisory put out by the bishops' conference declared, "Catholic respect for the integrity of Judaism and for the ongoing validity of God's irrevocable covenant with the Jewish people is solidly founded on our faith in the unshakable faithfulness of God's own word.... In no way can the beatification of Edith Stein be understood by Catholics as giving impetus to unwarranted proselytizing among the Jewish community. On the contrary, it urges us to ponder the continuing religious significance of Jewish traditions, with which we have so much in common, and to approach Jews not as potential 'objects' of conversion but rather as bearers of a unique witness to the Name of the One God, the God of Israel." Meditation on and emulation of St. Benedicta of the Cross, the advisory emphasized, "will deepen the faith of Catholics and, properly understood, should lead Catholics to a deeper appreciation of the spiritual richness and integrity of Judaism, the faith to which God has called the Jewish people" (Keeler, "Advisory").

Edith herself showed no inclination of proselytizing toward members of her own family. When her niece Lotte stopped for a visit at the Carmel in Cologne on her way to the United States, Edith handed the eighteen-year-old a little book as a keepsake of what she must have known would be their last time together. As Edith's niece Susanne Batzdorff points out, it is significant that the little book was neither a religious tract nor a missionary text, but rather a novella by Bjørnstjerne Bjørnssen, inscribed in German, *To dear Lotte, as a memento of her visit to Carmel.* "My aunt's choice of a farewell gift to her young niece also throws light on her disinclination to make any sort of missionary attempts toward members of her own family. Aunt Edith maintained her own right to profess her faith according to her conscience, but at the same time she would not presume to take unfair advantage of her loving relationship to practice missionary activity among her relatives" (*Aunt Edith*, 128).

A second concern noted in the bishops' advisory was that raising up a Jewish convert as symbolic of the six million victims might lead to an "appropriation" by the Church of the *Shoah* itself, making it seem that the Church, not the Jewish people, was the primary victim of Nazi genocide. "In honoring Edith Stein, the Church wishes to honor all the six million Jewish victims of the *Shoah.* Christian veneration of Edith Stein does not lessen but rather strengthens our need to preserve and honor the memory of the six million.... Catholic veneration of Edith Stein will necessarily contribute to a continuing and deepened examination of conscience regarding sins of commission and omission perpetrated by Christians against Jews during the dark years of World War II, as well as reflection on those Christians who risked their very lives to save their Jewish brothers and sisters.... Through Edith Stein the Church calls all Christians today to join with the Jewish people in opposing any and all forms of anti-Semitism."

Chapter 19

☞

In the Hands of Divine Providence

It is not a coincidence that Edith kept statements about her conversion to the Catholic Faith her "secret." As Michael Linssen, O.C.D., director of the then-Archivum Carmelitanum Edith Stein in Würzburg, Germany, noted:

Repeatedly Edith Stein writes that what happens interiorly to a person, in that person's life with God, remains hidden so that no one is to be informed of it. But she also says that the effects of God's grace cannot remain hidden. By associating with God, the human being grows toward his or her perfection. In this growing into oneself and toward God, one inevitably and irrevocably encounters the cross. This is "perhaps a quiet, life-long martyrdom of which no one has any idea," or more outwardly, "the person zealously striving for God's glory unfailingly evokes bitter opposition to this plan." Edith Stein saw through the events of the time before and during World War II. She foresaw the holocaust. She had a premonition of her end. It was precisely her hiddenness in God that gave her the confident inner rest and outer composure with which she understood it, to place it in perspective. (*Hidden Life*, preface)

Everything about Edith's life story, ultimately, became a genuine "testimony of love" that magnified God through her. She wrote about her faith: "When God reveals Himself as The One That Is, as Creator and Sustainer, and when the Redeemer says, 'He who believes in the Son has life eternal,' then these are all clear answers to the riddle of my own being" (*Daybook*, 60). She wrote about her Supreme Lover through whom she breathed, she loved, and had her being: "Love in its ultimate perfection is realized only in God: in the mutual love of the Divine Being, in self-surrendering divine existence. Love is God's being, God's life, God's nature. It corresponds to each of the divine persons and simultaneously to their unity." And she marveled at God's divine mercy: "Again and again I am filled with gratitude when I think of the marvelous and mysterious instances of God's providence in our lives" (ibid.).

Truly, Edith was a friend of Jesus, a faithful follower of the Jewish Master, who not only lived for Him but also died for Him. As Jesuit Father Jan H. Nota remarked:

Edith Stein's obedience to her conscience led her to travel on unaccustomed paths. If the Jewish people seem to stand alone again today, her life and martyrdom are clear testimony that God's election of her people is an enduring one. She was a woman who gave herself fully to this world, yet always remembered that she and her fellow human beings were on their way to God. She was a scholar of considerable philosophical output and a superb translator, who always remained a person of such great reserve and humility that, despite her accomplishments, most people never suspected the measure of her greatness. And yet, when it comes to philosophy and religion, what else but humility is the basic condition for the discovery of truth? (Herbstrith, *Edith Stein*, 13)

Everything that we know about Edith suggests "that Edith Stein was an unusually integrated person, capable of a high state of contemplative prayer," Hampl observes in her Stein essay. She "adapted naturally to the core of prayer: She understood her vocation as an act of solidarity (or, her old word, empathy) with the suffering of the world." When she entered Carmel, Edith chose to call herself "of the Cross" because "the Cross was where she stood. It was *her* mystery, and she made it her name. It was not for her an empty or merely edifying metaphor, but the image of shared, and ultimately redemptive, pain" (*Stories*, 120–121).

Edith's conversion to Christianity, similarly, is what led her to rediscover her Jewish roots and her belonging to the people of Israel, wrote the Carmelite Priors General, noting that their sister Edith, through her life and death, had the mission of acting as a bridge for Jewish-Christian dialogue.

In addition to her family ties, which grew stronger, there began to grow in her life of Christian faith the conviction that she had also been called to offer her suffering and life for her people.... Her love for her people and awareness of the mission that the Lord had given her grew even stronger when the persecution against Jews started to get more severe. She felt that her belonging to the chosen people united her to Christ not only spiritually but also by blood. She was convinced that the fate of her persecuted people was also her fate.... "And (I also trust) in the Lord's having accepted my life for all of them. I keep having to think

Edith Stein: St. Teresa Benedicta of the Cross

of Queen Esther who was taken from among her people precisely that she might represent them before the king. I am a very poor and powerless little Esther, but the King who chose me is infinitely great and merciful." (Maccise and Chalmers, "Losing to Win")

On October 1, 1999, Pope John Paul II proclaimed Edith Stein a co-patron saint of Europe — along with Catherine of Siena and Bridget of Sweden. The desire "to emphasize the important role that women have had and have in the ecclesial and civil history of the continent" led the Pope to make the proclamation during the opening Mass of the special assembly of the Synod of Bishops for Europe. Addressing the "disillusioned continent," for which regained political freedom at the close of the twentieth century has not brought happiness, the Holy Father urged, "Europe of the third millennium, do not give up, do not give in to discouragement, do not be resigned to ways of thinking and living that have no future, because they are not based on the firm certainty of the word of God."

In a unique way, Edith Stein is "a symbol of the dramas in Europe in our time." Edith's encounter with Christianity "did not lead her to reject her Jewish roots," the Pope wrote in his apostolic letter. "Rather it enabled her to fully discover them." Her entire life was "a kind of bridge" between her Jewish roots and her Christian faith. And her violent death remains a "proclamation of the Gospel of the cross, with which she identified herself." In proclaiming Edith Stein a patroness of all Europe, the Pope said he wanted "to raise on this continent a banner of respect, tolerance and acceptance" that invites all people to understand each other beyond ethnic, cultural, and religious differences. All three women, the Pope emphasized, are connected in a special

way with Europe's history and the continent's "many painful tri-
als ... during this hazardous and difficult century that is coming
to its end.... All three of them admirably express the synthesis
between contemplation and action. Their lives and their works
testify with great eloquence to the power of the risen Christ."
Through these new intercessors for the continent, "European
Christians and ecclesial communities of all confessions, as well
as European citizens and Nations, genuinely committed to the
quest for truth and the common good," will be able to be inspired
in this third millennium by the example of these three women.

Chapter 20

Edith Stein's Gift to the World

Edith Stein's journey of faith and her philosophy of thought parallel, in many ways, those of Karol Wojtyla, Pope John Paul II.

Like Pope John Paul II, Edith had deep interest in phenomenological philosophy and in St. Thomas Aquinas, pondering the connections between reason and faith. Edith became assistant to Edmund Husserl, the founder of phenomenology, the current of philosophy that the future Pope John Paul wrote about in his doctoral dissertation. Both the Pope and Edith devoted reflection to the vocation of woman in the modern world. And both were disciples of St. John of the Cross and the Carmelite tradition. Indeed, with her canonization, Sister Teresa Benedicta of the Cross became—along with her beloved Mother Teresa of Avila and Thérèse of Lisieux—another Teresa, who, as the Pope said, "takes her place among the host of saints who do honor to the Carmelite Order."

The Pope, who himself suffered under the Nazi occupation of his native Poland and grew up not far from the Auschwitz-Birkenau death camp, made improving relations with Jews a cornerstone of his pontificate. During his first trip to Poland as Pope in 1979, the Holy Father visited Auschwitz, Stein's place of death, becoming the first Pontiff to visit a concentration camp. In 1986, he also became the first Pope to enter and pray in a synagogue. It was during that visit to the Rome synagogue that the Pope first referred to Jews as Catholics' "older brothers" in faith.

We Remember: A Reflection on the Shoah, Pope John Paul II's 1998 document, was prepared for over eleven years by the Vatican's Commission for Religious Relations with Jews. Spearheaded by the Pope, the fourteen-page document opens with a prefatory letter by him that proclaims, "The crime which has become known as the *Shoah* remains an indelible stain on the history of the century that is coming to a close. It is my fervent hope," he continued, that the document will help "to heal the wounds of past misunderstanding and injustices."

In a momentous Jubilee Year pilgrimage to the Holy Land, Pope John Paul II publicly read a letter seeking forgiveness for acts committed against "the people of the Covenant." The letter, which the Pope placed into a crevice of Jerusalem's Western Wall on March 26, 2000, is on permanent display at Jerusalem's Yad Vashem Memorial of the Holocaust. The letter reads: "God of our fathers, you chose Abraham and his descendants to bring your Name to the Nations: we are deeply saddened by the behavior of those who in the course of history have caused these children of yours to suffer, and asking your forgiveness we wish to commit ourselves to genuine brotherhood with the people of the Covenant."

Edith Stein is pointed to "as a model of a woman of courage and intelligence, often paired with figures such as Dorothy Day as a model of one who had profound influence on the life of both the Church and of society. Surely," argued Dr. Fisher in his introduction to *Aunt Edith*, "this positive record since the beatification should be taken into account by those in the Jewish and Catholic communities who raised these quite legitimate concerns.... Many in the Jewish community ... may not agree with the Pope's understanding of Edith Stein as at once fully a Jew and fully a Catholic, but his very sensitive attempt to ensure that her memory will not be abused by Catholics to promote either Christian triumphalism or organized proselytism aimed at the Jews ... should be respected for its integrity within the context of Catholic belief" (*Aunt Edith*, 14, 16).

While agreeing that Jews and Christians have much to say to each other and much to do together, Professor David Novak, however, believes that Edith Stein represents "our impasse. She cannot be a bridge between Jews and Catholics because in this world one cannot be simultaneously both a faithful Jew and a faithful Catholic. Since the Jewish and Catholic communities are mutually exclusive, and both Jews and Catholics derive their identities from God's covenant with their communities, no member of one community can also be a member in good standing of the other." Moreover, he stresses, "one cannot expect the approval of the covenanted community one has left. As with Abraham our father, the answer to God's call always involves leaving some earlier household in one way or another, and that household does not and cannot provide one with a warm farewell" (Novak, "Edith Stein," 17).

Nonetheless, Dr. Freda Mary Oben, a noted speaker on Edith Stein and herself a convert from Judaism, sees Edith as a symbol of "the inherent unity between Judaism and Christianity and as a hopeful sign of their ensuing reconciliation." Edith Stein, she believes, "stands for the ten million people who were consumed in the flames of the crematoria: six million Jews and four million Christians" (*Edith Stein*, 77).

Edith Stein: St. Teresa Benedicta of the Cross

Only continued dialogue between Jews and Catholic Christians will promote Edith Stein as a true bridge rather than a stumbling block to Catholic-Jewish dialogue. As Stein's niece Susanne Batzdorff said, quoting a Passionist priest and a personal friend at a Washington, DC, seminar on Stein, "If Edith Stein can be the means of promoting fruitful dialogue between our two religions, she will have achieved a greater miracle than that for which she was canonized." Batzdorff then added, "I feel that the miracle can only be achieved by us—Christians and Jews, talking to each other, working together, and thus bringing about the progress we all say we desire."

Batzdorff, who attended both her Aunt Edith's beatification in 1987 and her canonization in 1998, said at the Washington, DC, conference that it was much easier to attend the canonization because in the intervening years "Pope John Paul II has managed to build bridges where hitherto unbridgeable gulfs had appeared." She cited as examples the Pope's role in removing the Carmelite convent from Auschwitz, his visit to the Rome synagogue, his establishment of Vatican-Israeli diplomatic relations, and his holding of a commemoration of the *Shoah* at the Vatican.

Ultimately, Edith's own family, some of them converts to Protestant Christianity, others to Catholicism, have very diverse views about their aunt and relative being recognized as a Catholic saint and of the symbolic meaning of her life and death. To her Protestant nephew, the late Gerhard Stein, Edith symbolizes to the world the Jewish people who perished. "Just as it is told that Jesus sacrificed his life for the sins of mankind, so Edith, according to reports, went consciously to her death by gas as a sacrifice for her beloved Jewish people." To others in the family, such as her nephew Ernst Ludwig Biberstein, to speak of Edith being martyred "in behalf of" her people is to imply she died for their atonement and salvation. "In that case, I could not allow myself to take part in this ceremony. That would be an almost blasphemous debasement of the sacrifice of the millions who, for the sake of their faith … went, like her, to a bestial death" (*Aunt Edith*, 204–205).

It is precisely this diversity, Batzdorff believes, that may be the "answer" to the questions raised by Catholics and Jews regarding Edith Stein's life and death. "In a small way, the family of Edith Stein mirrors the family of humankind. Just as the family of Edith Stein could come together in this setting, despite our different backgrounds and beliefs, so Jews and Christians can come together in an atmosphere of peace and good will, to open a dialogue, to reach some understanding and find a way to bridge our differences." Christians and Jews, she added, "have already come a long way toward closer rapprochement and better understanding, but our work is not finished. We must learn about each other's beliefs and ideology with open minds and mutual respect, conceding to each other the right to be different, to worship in our own ways" (ibid., 206, 210).

Chapter 21

⁀

Edith's Signature Phrase

Like a bird collecting twigs for its nest, a memoirist collects ideas, reflections, and images to create a foundation, a structure, that reflects the personal experiences of Edith Stein as author and as person. "Twigs" often included notebooks or journals, letters, a sketch pad. Often, without knowing why or expanding for whom, she will contemplate "out loud" on what many of us retain as secret thoughts: the blueness of the ocean, the name of a musical piece, or a memory of a person or event. As Patricia Hampl reflects in her essay "Red Sky in the Morning" (part of her own memoir collection, *I Could Tell You Stories*), memoirists want "to tell it *all*—the all of personal experience, of consciousness itself. That includes a story, but also the whole expanding universe of sensation and thought that flows beyond the confines of narrative and proves every life to be not only an isolated story line but a bit of the cosmos, spinning and streaming into the great, ungraspable pattern of existence. Memoirists wish to tell their mind, not their story." The gift they give us stems from the readers' own need for intimacy, Hampl notes. "More than a story, we want a voice speaking softly, urgently, in our ear. Which is to say, to our heart" (*Stories*, 18–19).

Edith Stein: St. Teresa Benedicta of the Cross

Edith Stein was once labeled by her family as "sealed with seven seals" because of her private nature. And she refused to discuss the impetus for her conversion, noting it as a private, secret matter. And yet, in a very real and honest way, Edith opened up her heart and allowed herself to be touched through her writing, especially through her memoirs and through her letters. Although Edith herself observed a rational and logical reason for writing the book that eventually became *Life in a Jewish Family*, Edith's honesty about herself and those around her in the narrative exposes her to readers in a manner that, perhaps, Edith herself never did otherwise.

Edith's letters, much in the same way, serve as a kind of epistolary journal in which she shares with her friends, family members, and former colleagues a piece of her heart that was not often exposed. It is here that we hear her courage, feel her frustration, and find her humor. Her letters reveal the pain of being misunderstood and confess the recognition of her probable destiny. It is in her letters that we learn of Edith's innermost thoughts, her anguish and her concern for her mother, her thankfulness for a friend's honest critique, her hopes and prayers for her family as they scatter all over the world. Edith's letters also reveal and illustrate her character traits. She was courageous, honest, direct, faithful, dedicated, realistic, spiritual, and above all, prayerful.

In a letter written in April of 1931 — her final year of teaching at St. Magdalena's in Speyer — to Benedictine Sister Adelgundis Jaegerschmid of Freiburg-Günterstal, Edith remarked with earnest honesty that, although people continually demanded "clever themes" of her as a lecturer, her lecturer's platform — her orator's *Ceterum censeo* — came down to "a small, simple truth that I have to express: *How to go about living at the Lord's hand*" (*Self-Portrait*, 87).

This is Edith Stein's signature phrase.

For this professional and highly educated young woman, who for so many years climbed the academic ladder of recognition and prestige, all of life came down to a small, simple fact more real than anything she could touch. She believed in divine providence, and she put herself completely, wholeheartedly, into God's hands. "To be a child of God," Edith noted, "means to walk at the hand of God, to do God's will, to put all worries and all hopes in God's hands.... God in us, and we in Him, that is our portion in the divine realm for which the incarnation laid the foundation" (*Daybook*, 118, 121).

For this reason, it is critical that as we remember Edith Stein and learn from her life and her writings, we also meditate on her name. "Why do we continue to refer to Sr. Benedicta of the Cross as Edith Stein?" asks Carmelite Sister Ruth Miriam Irey. "She was known in Germany as a writer, philosopher, speaker and feminist—but would the world have either known or remembered Edith Stein had she not died as Sr. Benedicta? To the Nazis, it was the 'Jew' Edith Stein that was killed at Auschwitz. For the Church it was Sr. Benedicta of the Cross. 'Of the Cross' ... was her identity and destiny.... If her name was so important to her, why is it not as important to us?... As a Catholic, she offered her life in the hope that her suffering and death would be redemptive.... If we fail to use the Cross, either in itself or in her name, for whom is Edith Stein a martyr?" ("Sister Benedicta," 27). As Sister Ruth Miriam concludes, "Edith Stein was murdered because she was a Jew. However, Sr. Benedict of the Cross also died because she was ... [a] Catholic who chose to offer her life and share in the fate of her *people* in atonement as a victim of peace. Sr. Benedicta allowed the form of the Cross to form her. In her life and works, she reflected the life of Christ and showed how these two elements *melt into the most complete unity under the sign of the Cross*" (ibid., 29).

There are no coincidences. Certainly, Edith's choice of a subtitle for her Carmelite name, "of the Cross," had unmeasurable significance for this mystic, contemplative woman. But it was also a great grace—a mysterious preparation—that it was the work of John of the Cross that occupied Edith for the final months of her life. "I tried to make a copy of the sketch our Holy Father John made on a piece of paper about 5 cm. in size, after the vision he had of the Crucified at the Monastery of the Incarnation. The reproduction of it in P. Bruno's book is not exactly sharp, and I am anything but an artist. But I made it with great reverence and love," she wrote in a letter a few months before her death. "Because of the work I am doing [*The Science of the Cross*] I live almost constantly immersed in thoughts about our Holy Father John. That is a great grace" (*Self-Portrait*, 339). And in December 1941, she wrote, "A *scientia crucis* (knowledge of the Cross) can be gained only when one comes to feel the Cross radically. I have been convinced of that from the first moment and have said, from my heart: *Ave*, Crux, *spes unica!* (Hail Cross, our only hope!)" (ibid., 341).

"Only those who are saved, only children of grace, can in fact be bearers of Christ's cross," Edith once wrote. "Only in union with the divine Head does human suffering take on expiatory power. To suffer and to be happy although suffering, to have one's feet on the earth, to walk on the dirty and rough paths of this earth and yet to be enthroned with Christ at the Father's right hand, to laugh and cry with the children of this world and ceaselessly sing the praises of God with the choirs of angels—this is the life of the Christian until the morning of eternity breaks forth" (*Hidden Life*, 93).

Edith's Signature Phrase

Edith Stein teaches us "that love for Christ undergoes suffering," Pope John Paul II noted at her canonization. "The mystery of the Cross gradually enveloped her whole life, spurring her to the point of making the supreme sacrifice. As a bride on the Cross, Sr. Teresa Benedicta did not only write profound pages about the 'Science of the Cross,' but was thoroughly trained in the school of the Cross.... Faith and the Cross proved inseparable to her. Having matured in the school of the Cross, she found the roots to which the tree of her own life was attached. She understood that it was very important for her 'to be a daughter of the chosen people and to belong to Christ not only spiritually, but also through blood.'"

The depth of the divine mystery became perceptible to Edith in the silence of contemplation, the Pope noted. Gradually, "as she grew in the knowledge of God, worshiping him in spirit and truth, she experienced ever more clearly her specific vocation to ascend the Cross with Christ, to embrace it with serenity and trust, to love it by following in the footsteps of her beloved Spouse."

Perhaps one of Edith's greatest legacies to the body of believers is her own devotion to prayer. Edith understood every person's need for still, quiet prayer. "We need those hours in which we listen silently and let the divine word work within us," she wrote (*Daybook*, 121). After her baptism but before entering the Carmelites, even with her busy teaching and speaking schedule, Edith sought constant opportunities to pray. It is precisely people with many obligations and who are fully involved, she argued, who need such communion with God in inner stillness. Edith the scholar, the philosopher, the theologian, the spiritual giant, the feminist, and finally, the martyr, teaches us that we do not need to be in a church to be still with God in

Edith Stein: St. Teresa Benedicta of the Cross

prayer. We can—and need to—catch our breath spiritually anywhere, constantly. We, too, are "*in via*," "on the way," she wrote from within the convent's walls, "for Carmel is a high mountain that one must climb from its very base. But it is a tremendous grace to go this way." Of her personal vocation to contemplative prayer, Edith added, "Whoever enters Carmel is not lost to his own, but is theirs fully for the first time; it is our vocation to stand before God for all." She went on, "And, believe me, in the hours of prayer I always remember especially those who would like to be in my position. Please help me that I may become worthy to live in the inner sanctum of the church and to represent those who must labor outside" (*Self-Portrait*, 154, 177–178).

Her communal death at Auschwitz's gas chambers and crematoria prevents us from honoring her remains, her individuality, in the same manner we naturally remember and honor countless other holy men and women. Ultimately, Sister Teresa Benedicta of the Cross would probably prefer that there be no memorial grave or relic in her honor. Yet those of us who turn to her for an example on how to live a life of surrender to God's providence still have a unique and incomparable relic of her spirit: her prolific writings as a reflection of her faith. They are her true legacy. As Edith wrote in 1931 to a friend on the eve of her baptism, "That is how it ought to be; that, without any kind of human assurance, you place yourself totally in God's hands, then all the deeper and more beautiful will be the security attained. My wish for your Baptismal Day and for all of your future life is that you may find the fullness of God's peace" (ibid., 105).

It is precisely this spiritual awareness that makes Edith Stein "a model to inspire us and a protectress to call upon. We give thanks to God for this gift," Pope John Paul II proclaimed at her canonization. "May the new saint be an example to us in our commitment to serve freedom, in our search for the truth. May her witness constantly strengthen the bridge of mutual understanding between Jews and Christians."

Edith Stein, Sister Teresia Benedicta a Cruce, pray for us!

"To God, the Father"
by Sister Teresa Benedicta of the Cross
(This poem is assumed to have been written in 1939, possibly for a memorial service for the dead [see *Selected Writings*, 81].)

Bless the mind deeply troubled
Of the sufferers,
The heavy loneliness of profound souls
The restlessness of human beings,
The sorrow which no soul ever confides
To a sister soul.

And bless the passage of moths at night,
Who do not shun specters on paths unknown.
Bless the distress of men
Who die within the hour,
Grant them, loving God, a peaceful, blessed end.

Bless all the hearts, the clouded ones, Lord, above all,
Bring healing to the sick.
To those in torture, peace.
Teach those who had to carry their beloved to the
    grave, to forget.
Leave none in agony of guilt on all the earth.

Edith Stein: St. Teresa Benedicta of the Cross

Bless the joyous ones, O Lord, and keep them under
    your wing.
My mourning clothes You never yet removed.
At times my tired shoulders bear a heavy burden.
But give me strength, and I'll bear it
In penitence to the grave.

Then bless my sleep, the sleep of all the dead.
Remember what Your son suffered for me in agony
    of death.
Your great mercy for all human needs
Gives rest to all the dead in Your eternal peace.

Chapter 22

＾

A Natural Journey with Edith

Much before Edith's life and her faith were officially recognized by
the Church as an example for the community of believers in the
Church Militant, those of us still walking the journey to heaven,
there already existed a spontaneous, popular cult — private altars,
church memorials, works of art — dedicated to Edith. St. Martin's Church in Bergzabern, for example, the church where Edith
Stein was baptized in 1922, is devoted to her memory. Cards of
the church are issued bearing her name. On the wall adjacent to
the baptismal font, a plaque is dedicated to her. A street by the
church is called Edith Stein Strasse. Even the youth building,
the Edith Stein House, was constructed in her honor. In her native Breslau — a city that became Wroclaw, Poland, following the
end of the war — the Edith Stein chapel in St. Michael's Church
includes a container embedded in the altar's foundation, which
is filled with earth from the death camp at Auschwitz-Birkenau,
where she died in 1942. Nearby, a sculptured stack of manuscripts
illustrates that Edith Stein was a prolific author during her lifetime. The historical museum, located in the city's town hall, holds
a bust of Edith Stein among other famous sons and daughters of
the city of Breslau (Wroclaw). And at St. Ludgeri Church in

Edith Stein: St. Teresa Benedicta of the Cross

Münster, Germany, a plaque on the wall by a large iron cross commemorates the thirteen hours of prayer that Edith Stein spent there as she made her extraordinary decision to enter Carmel.

On August 9, 1982, the fortieth anniversary of her death, Edith Stein was honored and remembered on radio and television broadcasts, in books, periodicals, newspapers, and by memorial services. As Sister Waltraud Herbstrith, of the Edith Stein Carmel in Tübingen, notes in the foreword to her Stein biography, "Throughout Germany she has come to be acknowledged as a model and inspiration; today there are schools, institutes, libraries, community centers, student residences, streets, and public squares all bearing her name" (*Edith Stein*, 7). Even the German Postal Service issued a commemorative stamp of Stein in 1983, showing her dressed in her Carmelite habit.

Likewise, cities peripheral to Edith's life "fell in love not just with Edith but with her ancestors as well," observed Stein's niece Susanne Batzdorff. Lubliniec (or Lublinitz, as it was called when still in Germany) was where Edith's grandfather Solomon Courant had a grocery business and where much of the family lived. As children, Batzdorff's mother — Edith's sister Erna — and Edith used to go there for summer vacation. "The street where the Courant house stands has been named after Edith Stein. Today the walls in my great-grandfather's home are covered with charts, a family tree, photographs and other paraphernalia from the life of Edith and her relatives. School children in Lubliniec are encouraged to write about Edith Stein, to create paintings and collages that link her to their town, making her a sort of patron saint of their city."[29]

---

[29] Susanne Batzdorff, "Tracing Edith Stein's Past," *America* (November 25, 1995): 12–17.

A Natural Journey with Edith

In October 1998, prior to Stein's canonization, an exposition in Ghent, Belgium, collected a large sampling of items that had over the decades emerged out of this popular devotion to this holy woman. Put together by Carmelite Father Frans Hoorn-aert, O.C.D., and Dr. Ilse Kerremans of the International Edith Stein Institute of Würzburg, the Edith Stein Exposition in Ghent was an extraordinary assembly of articles from all over Europe. There were many of Stein's original papers and manuscripts, first editions of some of her books, her own personal library, fam-ily photos, personal items, letters to her family and her friends, holy cards with handwritten notes. But the exposition, which Father Frans noted "brings Edith's spirituality to the people," also brought together art and artifacts by ordinary people in celebration of Edith Stein's life — among them, a painting from Cologne, a wood carving from Prague, a watercolor from Echt, images of stained-glass windows, charcoal sketches, a terracotta bust, oil paintings, a metal-and-wood sculpture, and holy cards. Some of these items featured Edith Stein. Some highlighted a certain moment in Stein's life, such as her baptism. Others mixed a symbol of her Carmelite spirituality with one representing her life, like a Star of David with the traditional Carmelite brown.

Without a doubt, the Church in Europe remembered Edith Stein.

It is not hard to explain why.

The Second Vatican Council noted, "It is supremely fitting that we love those friends and fellow heirs of Jesus Christ, who are also our brothers and extraordinary benefactors, that we ren-der due thanks to God for them and 'suppliantly invoke them and have recourse to their prayers, their power and help in obtaining benefits from God through his Son, Jesus Christ, our Lord, who is our sole Redeemer and Savior.' For by its very nature every genuine testimony of love which we show to those in heaven tends towards and terminates in Christ, who is the 'crown of all saints.' Through him it tends toward and terminates in God, who is wonderful in his saints and is magnified in them."[30]

Much of what we have in terms of the bulk of Edith's letters and original drafts has been due to the care and interest of the extended family Edith so loved. In a special way, her friend and closest-in-age sister, Erna Biberstein, saw her task as providing factual information wherever possible on her sister. Although she was "not dazzled by the prospect of sainthood for Edith," notes Erna's daughter, Erna saw herself as the guardian against misrepresentation and distortion of facts in the transmittal of Edith's life story, a task taken up after Erna's 1978 death by her daughter Susanne Batzdorff. Batzdorff's own recently published personal account, *Aunt Edith: The Jewish Heritage of a Catholic Saint*, provides an exceptional and familiar perspective into Edith's Jewishness—as well as access to material not found elsewhere.

Nothing short of divine providence led Edith's Carmelite community throughout Europe to recognize her unique gifts from the time she joined the convent. After the war, numerous people contacted the Carmelites to inquire about Edith—many of them former students from Speyer or Münster. This led the cloistered nuns who had known Edith and those familiar with her work to begin to collect the pieces of manuscripts and copies of her written legacy that had survived—essays, letters, stories, studies in philosophy. Then began the reconstruction and eventual publication of much of her typed and handwritten work, first in her native German, then in Spanish, English, and other languages.

---

[30] Second Vatican Council, Dogmatic Constitution on the Church *Lumen Gentium*, November 21, 1964, no. 50.

Even her most noteworthy philosophical writings, such as *Finite and Eternal Being*, never made it to print in her lifetime. The manuscript had been set for publication by Borgmeyer in 1936, but anti-Jewish laws prevented completion of the project and eventually the plates were destroyed.

We get a vivid sense of the tranquil life of the Stein family before the First World War, thanks to Edith's memoir, which she began writing in April 1933 and which remained unfinished, although she worked on it intermittently after her transfer to Holland. How the manuscript of her family's biography survived was truly providential. When the Nazis occupied Holland in early 1940, Edith feared an unexpected search of the Echt monastery by the Gestapo. A manuscript about life in a Jewish family would not only be readily destroyed, but it would also compromise the Sisters for sheltering the author. According to the testimonial account of Sister Pia, a member of the Echt community (as recounted by the translator of *Life in a Jewish Family*), Sister Pia and Edith buried the entire manuscript in the ground "very near to the cemetery," but within the monastery enclosure (see *Life*, 463). The manuscript remained buried for three months until Edith dug it up again, afraid that it would be damaged or destroyed in the moist ground. Sister Pia recounts that, taking pity on Edith's plight, "she took it upon herself to locate a safe hiding place for the manuscript in the monastery" (ibid.). When the Echt community had to evacuate the building during the war, many of the valuable articles from the library and the sacristy were walled up in a basement room, but the manuscript was not among them. It was in 1945, and only after Sister Pia heard that the building was going to be used as the quarantine quarters for hundreds of people who were being repatriated in Holland from labor camps, that Sister Pia went to Echt to retrieve the manuscript from the unnamed hiding place. She then entrusted the manuscript to the Provincial of the Dutch Carmelites, and, through him, the two packages eventually reached the Husserl Archive (see ibid.).

The German text of what became *Life in a Jewish Family* was posthumously published, initially in abridged form, in 1965. Thanks to the Institute of Carmelite Studies, based in Washington, DC, an English translation by Sister Josephine Koeppel, O.C.D., of the Elysburg, Pennsylvania, Carmel, was published in 1986. Edith Stein's work, in fact, continues to be published as it is translated by ICS Publications, the Washington province of the Discalced Carmelites.

For their continued preservation, work, and reproduction of Edith's books, essays, and letters, we owe the worldwide Carmelite community a world of thanks.

Works Consulted

Adler, David A. *We Remember the Holocaust*. New York: Scholastic, 1989.

Batzdorff, Susanne. *Aunt Edith: The Jewish Heritage of a Catholic Saint*. Springfield, IL: Templegate, 1998.

———. *Edith Stein: Selected Writings*. Springfield, IL: Templegate, 1990.

———. "Tracing Edith Stein's Past." *America* (November 25, 1995): 12–17.

Brenner, Rachel Feldhay. *Writing as Resistance: Four Women Confronting the Holocaust*. University Park, PA: Pennsylvania State University Press, 1997.

Carroll, James. "The Saint and the Holocaust." *New Yorker* (June 7, 1999): 52–57.

De Fabregues, Jean. *Edith Stein: Philosopher, Carmelite Nun, Holocaust Martyr*. Boston: St. Paul Books and Media, 1965.

Feister, John Bookser. "Edith Stein: Our Newest Saint." *St. Anthony Messenger* (October 1998): 22–26.

Garcia, Laura. "Edith Stein—Convert, Nun, Martyr." *Crisis* (June 1997): 18–23.

Gay, Ruth. *The Jews of Germany: A Historical Portrait*. New Haven: Yale University Press, 1992.

Graef, Hilda C. *The Scholar and the Cross: The Life and Work of Edith Stein*. Westminster, MD: Newman Press, 1955.

Hampl, Patricia. *I Could Tell You Stories: Sojourns in the Land of Memory*. New York: W. W. Norton, 1999.

Herbstrith, Waltraud, O.C.D. *Edith Stein: A Biography*. San Francisco: Ignatius Press, 1985.

Herbstrith, Waltraud, O.C.D., ed. *Never Forget: Christian and Jewish Perspectives on Edith Stein*. Washington, DC: ICS Publications, 1998.

Hillesum, Etty. *An Interrupted Life: The Diaries, 1941–1943 and Letters from Westerbork*. New York: Henry Holt, 1996.

Hitler, Adolf. *Hitler: Sämtliche Aufzeichnungen 1905–1924*. Edited by Eberhard Jäckel. Translated by Peter Keupen. Stuttgart: Deutsche Verlags-Anstalt, 1980.

Irey, Ruth Miriam, O.C.D. "Sister Benedicta of the Cross (Edith Stein): Her Faith, Her Philosophy, Her People." Unpublished essay, 1998.

Jäckel, Eberhard. *Hitler's World View: A Blueprint for Power*. Cambridge: Harvard University Press, 1981.

Maccise, P. Camilo, O.C.D., and Joseph Chalmers, O.Carm. "Losing to Win: The Journey of Bl. Teresa Benedicta of the Cross." August 9, 1998. http://www.helpfellowship.org/Edith/ Edith_Stein_1998.htm.

Works Consulted

Mendes-Flohr, Paul. *German Jews: A Dual Identity*. New Haven, CT: Yale University Press, 1999.

Neyer, Maria Amata, O.C.D. *Edith Stein: Her Life in Photos and Documents*. Washington, DC: ICS Publications, 1999.

Novak, David. "Edith Stein, Apostate Saint." *First Things* (October 1999): 15–17.

Oben, Freda Mary, Ph.D. *Edith Stein: Scholar, Feminist, Saint*. Staten Island, NY: Alba House, 1988.

Pulzer, Peter. *Jews and the German State: The Political History of a Minority, 1848–1933*. Oxford: Blackwell, 1992.

"St. Teresa Benedicta of the Cross—Edith Stein" (1998). Posted on the website of the Discalced Carmelites. http://www.ocd. pcn.net/ed_en.htm.

Sawicki, Marianne. *Body, Text and Science: The Literacy of Investigative Practices and the Phenomenology of Edith Stein*. Boston: Kluwer, 1997.

———. "Decision and Spontaneity in the Pre-Baptismal Philosophy of Edith Stein." Public lecture given at St. John's University, New York, October 14, 1998.

Sokolowski, Robert. *Introduction to Phenomenology*. Cambridge: Cambridge University Press, 2000.

Stein, Edith. *An Edith Stein Daybook: To Live at the Hand of the Lord*. Translated by Susanne Batzdorff. Springfield, IL: Templegate, 1994.

———. *Essays on Woman*. Translated by Freda Mary Oben. Washington, DC: ICS Publications, 1996.

―――. *The Hidden Life: Hagiographic Essays, Meditations, Spiritual Texts*. Edited by L. Gelber and Michael Linssen, O.C.D. Translated by Waltraut Stein. Washington, DC: ICS Publications, 1992.

―――. *Knowledge and Faith*. Walter Redmond, trans. Washington, D.C.: ICS Publications, 2000.

―――. *Life in a Jewish Family: Her Unfinished Autobiographical Account*. Edited by L. Gelber and Romaeus Leuven, O.C.D. Translated by Josephine Koeppel, O.C.D. Washington, DC: ICS Publications, 1986.

―――. *On the Problem of Empathy*. Translated by Waltraut Stein. Washington, DC: ICS Publications, 1989.

―――. *Self-Portrait in Letters: 1916–1942*. Edited by L. Gelber and Romaeus Leuven, O.C.D. Translated by Josephine Koeppel, O.C.D. Washington, DC: ICS Publications, 1993.

Sullivan, John, O.C.D., S.T.D., ed. *Holiness Befits Your House: Canonization of Edith Stein: A Documentation*. Washington, DC: ICS Publications, 2000.

See also:

Discalced Carmelite Order homepage: www.ocd.pcn.net/index_en.htm

The Hidden Life: http://www.meditationsfromcarmel.com/content/volume-iv

Publishing house of the Institute of Carmelite Studies [ICS], Discalced Carmelite Friars, Washington, DC: www.icspublications.org

Works Consulted

"The Life and Texts of Edith Stein," collection of links by the Carmelite Nuns of Baltimore: http://www.baltimorecarmel. org/saints/Stein/edith%20stein%20index.htm

Chronology of Writings of Edith Stein (1891–1942), Hesburgh Libraries, University of Notre Dame: http://library.nd.edu/ colldev/subject_home_pages/catholic/sawickibibstein.shtml

"The Phenomenology of Edith Stein," abridged lecture by Dr. Marianne Sawicki, St. John's University, New York, October 15, 1998: http://library.nd.edu/colldev/subject_home_pages/ catholic/personal_connections.shtml

Special Acknowledgments

Special thanks go to the following for the use of their material in this work:

Susanne Batzdorff, *Aunt Edith: The Jewish Heritage of a Catholic Saint* and *Edith Stein: Selected Writings* (Springfield, IL: Templegate Publishers, 1998 and 1990).

Ruth Gay, *The Jews of Germany* (New Haven, CT: Yale University Press, 1992).

Waltraud Herbstrith, *Edith Stein: A Biography*, Copyright © 1971 by Verlagsgesellschaft Gerhard Kaffke mbh, Ashaffenburg. English translation © 1985 by Harper and Row, Publishers, Inc. Reprinted by permission of HarperCollins Publishers, Inc.

Freda Mary Oben, Ph.D., *Edith Stein: Scholar, Feminist, Saint* (Staten Island, NY: Alba House, 1988).

Etty Hillesum: An Interrupted Life: The Diaries, 1941–1943 and Letters from Westerbork, © 1983 by Jonathan Cape Ltd. for English language translation of *An Interrupted Life*; © 1986 by Random House, Inc., for English language translation of *Letters from Westerbork*. Reprinted by permission of Henry Holt and Company.

Edith Stein: St. Teresa Benedicta of the Cross

Patricia Hampl, *I Could Tell You Stories: Sojourns in the Land of Memory*, Copyright © 1999 by Patricia Hampl. Used by permission of W. W. Norton and Company, Inc.

Excerpts from the following have been reprinted by permission of ICS Publications, Washington, D.C.:

Never Forget: Christian and Jewish Perspectives on Edith *Stein*, ed. Waltraud Herbstrith, O.C.D. (Washington, DC: ICS Publications, 1998).

Maria Amata Neyer, O.C.D., *Edith Stein: Her Life* in *Photos and Documents* (Washington, DC: ICS Publications, 1999).

Edith Stein, *Essays on Woman*, trans. Freda Mary Oben (Washington, DC: ICS Publications, 1996).

Edith Stein, *The Hidden Life: Hagiographic Essays, Meditations, Spiritual Texts*, ed. L. Gelber and Michael Linssen, O.C.D., trans. Waltraut Stein (Washington, DC: ICS Publications, 1992).

Edith Stein, *Knowledge and Faith*, trans. Walter Redmond (Washington, DC: ICS Publications, 2000).

Edith Stein, *Life in a Jewish Family: Her Unfinished Autobiographical Account*, ed. L. Gelber and Romaeus Leuven, O.C.D., trans. Josephine Koeppel, O.C.D. (Washington, DC: ICS Publications, 1986).

Edith Stein, *On the Problem of Empathy*, trans. Waltraut Stein (Washington, DC: ICS Publications, 1989).

Edith Stein, *Self-Portrait in Letters: 1916–1942*, by Edith Stein, edited by L. Gelber and Romaeus Leuven, O.C.D., translated by Josephine Koeppel, O.C.D. Washington, D.C.: ICS Publications, 1993.

John Sullivan, O.C.D., S.T.D., ed., *Holiness Befits Your House: Canonization of Edith Stein: A Documentation* (Washington, DC: ICS Publications, 2000).

Special Acknowledgments

With the exception of the photograph showing Edith Stein holding her cousin's son, the pictures appearing in this work, which are taken from *Edith Stein: Her Life in Photos and Documents*, are used by permission of ICS Publications, Washington, DC. The picture of Edith and her cousin's son is used by permission of the Edith Stein Archiv, Cologne.

Index

Index

Philosophical Society (Göttingen), 58

Pius XII, Pope, 172

Pius XI, Pope, 172

R

Red Cross, 61, 62, 63, 65, 151, 155, 162

Reinach, Adolf, 61, 68, 125

Reinach, Anna (Stettenheimer), 68, 69

Reinach, Pauline, 69

S

Scheler, Max, 50, 55, 56, 70

Schwind, Monsignor Josef (spiritual director), 79, 96

Second World War, 6, 13, 91, 131, 134, 172, 181, 183

Shoah, xiii, xvi, 159, 165, 166, 168, 176, 177, 180, 190, 192

Silesia, 13, 37, 151

Speyer, 79, 83, 96, 98, 117, 143, 144, 196, 206

Stein, Arno (brother), 109, 155

Stein, Auguste (née Courant) (mother), 13, 14, 15, 17, 18, 19, 20, 39, 40, 54, 62, 117, 118, 127

Stein, Elfriede "Frieda" (sister), 24, 146, 155, 176

Stein, Else (sister), 23, 41, 108, 110

Stein, Erna (sister), 23, 41, 43

Stein, Eva (niece), 155, 176

Stein, Gerhard (nephew), 192

Stein, Gertrude (sister-in-law), 146

Stein, Paul (brother), 22, 146, 155, 176

Stein, Rosa (sister), 5, 66, 71, 106, 108, 117, 123, 133, 137, 138, 142, 143, 144, 147, 149, 150, 151, 152, 153, 155, 160, 169, 176, 177, 178

Stein, Siegfried (father), 14, 15

T

Teresa, 76, 77, 78, 97, 98, 102, 103, 113, 114, 130, 131, 189

Teresa of Avila, 75

Thérèse of Lisieux, 102, 114, 189

Theresienstadt, 146, 147, 155

Third Reich, 37, 129, 143, 146, 170

Tübingen, xvii, 204

Tworoger, Elfriede "Frieda" (née Stein) (*see also under* Stein), 146, 155

W

Walzer, Father Raphael (spiritual director), 96, 102

Weil, Simone, 91

Westerbork (Holland), 147, 148, 149, 150, 153, 156, 160, 161, 167, 168

World War II (*see also* Second World War), 131, 172, 181, 183

World War I (*see also* First World War), 63

Y

Yom Kippur (Day of Atonement), 13, 20

Sophia Institute

Sophia Institute is a nonprofit institution that seeks to nurture the spiritual, moral, and cultural life of souls and to spread the Gospel of Christ in conformity with the authentic teachings of the Roman Catholic Church.

Sophia Institute Press fulfills this mission by offering translations, reprints, and new publications that afford readers a rich source of the enduring wisdom of mankind.

Sophia Institute also operates two popular online Catholic resources: CrisisMagazine.com and CatholicExchange.com.

Crisis Magazine provides insightful cultural analysis that arms readers with the arguments necessary for navigating the ideological and theological minefields of the day. *Catholic Exchange* provides world news from a Catholic perspective as well as daily devotionals and articles that will help you to grow in holiness and live a life consistent with the teachings of the Church.

In 2013, Sophia Institute launched Sophia Institute for Teachers to renew and rebuild Catholic culture through service to Catholic education. With the goal of nurturing the spiritual, moral, and cultural life of souls, and an abiding respect for the role and work of teachers, we strive to provide materials and programs that are at once enlightening to the mind and ennobling to the heart; faithful and complete, as well as useful and practical.

Sophia Institute gratefully recognizes the Solidarity Association for preserving and encouraging the growth of our apostolate over the course of many years. Without their generous and timely support, this book would not be in your hands.

www.SophiaInstitute.com
www.CatholicExchange.com
www.CrisisMagazine.com
www.SophiaInstituteforTeachers.org

Sophia Institute Press® is a registered trademark of Sophia Institute. Sophia Institute is a tax-exempt institution as defined by the Internal Revenue Code, Section 501(c)(3). Tax I.D. 22-2548708.